Three-Dog Nights:
The Search and Rescue of
Annette Poitras

By

A. K. Bruinn

and

Marcel Poitras

Edited by M. Harrison

© 2018 A. K. Bruinn

This book is dedicated to Search and Rescue personnel and First Responders worldwide.

Foreword

For a Search and Rescue volunteer, every SAR task starts the same – with an urgent alert from your cell phone that someone is in trouble. When we respond, we never know what to expect. On Monday, November 20th, 2017, I happened to be the Coquitlam SAR manager who took the initial call for a missing dog walker on Westwood Plateau in Coquitlam. This was the 50th call we had responded to in our team's busiest year.

What I had initially thought would be a simple search, over in a few hours, turned into our largest response in the last five years. It involved every member of our team, volunteers from 18 SAR groups from all over British Columbia, many first responders, and concerned members of the Tri-Cities community.

Being in charge of the search for the first 8 hours, and then assisting with the response over the next few days, I had very few opportunities to step back and reflect on what was happening. Even when the search was over, the team was engaged in cleaning up, and returning to normal life. This book is the first time I've had the chance to hear the full story of what happened over those days from the most important people in the story: Marcel and Annette.

Reading this book brought tears to my eyes. Hearing about Annette's and Marcel's ordeals through their own words brought a perspective on those events that I've rarely had access to. Author Anne Bruinn has managed to capture the essence of this amazing story of survival, with all it's small details – something that can be all too easy for a SAR responder to take for granted.

I lived through this event, and I *thoroughly* enjoyed reading it, and I feel you will too. Thanks to Marcel, Annette, and Anne for telling this story.

-      Michael Coyle, SAR Manager,
Coquitlam Search and Rescue

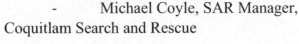

Michael Coyle (left) and Bill Papove (right)

Preface

This book was written at my request. As a mother with a degree in forestry and a dog-centred family business, this story hit home. Not only Annette's side resonated with me, but also the emotional struggle of the family left behind. I knew it was a story others would want to hear too.

I sent a Facebook message to Annette and Marcel asking if they would be interested in telling their story. After a sit-down meeting between the three of us, we decided Marcel and I would collaborate to write the book. The Poitras' opened their home to me, and I lived in their home's lower suite for eight days to complete the majority of the book. Marcel and Annette provided the details and I wove it into a story.

Without the support of my wonderful family, this book would still be on chapter six. Thank you for allowing me to abandon you for a week, and for welcoming me home with such aplomb! It turns out, the kids CAN do things for themselves, and my husband CAN keep the children thriving without me!

Thank you to my amazing friend Mary Harrison, who took time out of her crazy busy life to edit every page. Not only are you a brilliant editor, actor, singer, mother, and all around great human being, you are also the sister I never had. I love you dearly.

Also thank you to Michael Coyle at Coquitlam SAR for being available with resources and information, and Jon Lavoie for allowing us to include his beautiful photos.

Finally, thank you to Annette and Marcel for reaching deep and reliving these traumatic events. With release comes healing, and I hope writing it all down has given you some peace.

Introduction

These events occurred in Coquitlam, British Columbia, Canada. Coquitlam is one of 21 municipalities which make up Metro Vancouver. It is nestled against the Coast Mountains, with Burke Mountain, Eagle Ridge, and Coquitlam Mountain forming its northern boundary[1]. The area has a mild oceanic climate, with mean daily temperatures in November ranging from 3.8 degrees Celsius (38 degrees Farenheit) to 6.4 degrees Celsius (43 degrees Farenheit.)[1]

November is the rainiest month of the year, averaging 303 cms (12 inches) of rain over the 30 days[1]. This particular week in November, the city had braced for a Pineapple Express, which would bring heavy rains with the Hawaiian air currents.

On the first night, November 20th, the lowest temperature recorded was 2 degrees Celsius[2], the coldest night of the previous ten days. The second night, the warmer temperatures brought in by the Pineapple Express were a milder 9 degrees, contributing to Annette's survival.

As Annette was disoriented and had no sense of time, all times listed in her chapters are approximate. Conversations are borne of vague memories, elaborated for effect.

These are the conversations and events as Annette and Marcel recall them.

The term "three dog night" is said to be a phrase purportedly used by Australian Aborigines meaning "a night so cold you need to take three dogs to bed with you to stay warm."[3]

Pictures of SAR equipment, crews, and a description of this and other rescues can be found on the Coquitlam SAR website: www.coquitlam-sar.bc.ca/

The authors will be donating partial proceeds from sales of this book to the Coquitlam SAR.

[1] – geographic, temperature, and precipitation information taken from Wikipedia

[2] – temperature recordings taken from timeanddate.com

[3] – Urban Dictionary: three dog night at urbandictionary.com

Location Maps

Map of the general area showing the locations of key places. Source: QtheMap, City of Coquitlam. Coquitlam.ca

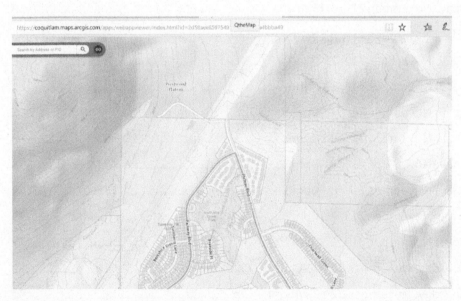

Map showing the end of Plateau Blvd, the access road, and the powerline clearing (white.) Source: QtheMap, City of Coquitlam, Coquitlam.ca

Contents

Day 1:

Monday, November 20th

Annette came in from the chilly November air, kicked off her wet hiking boots and rain jacket, then said to the girls, "Well that was a wet one! Let's grab some lunch before we head out again." She put the boots to dry on the drying mat by the door and hung her coat on a peg above it.

Chloe, Annette's black and white border collie and the eldest of the two dogs, headed straight for the water bowl in the laundry room. She was 5 years old and knew the routine well – a drink, a snack, and a quick nap before they went back out for their afternoon hike.

Roxy, a 2-year-old tan boxer she walked 3 to 4 times each week, was much more interested in what Annette was going to do now. Annette patted her on her head and said, "Have a drink Roxy, we'll go back out in an hour." Roxy trotted to the water bowl by the laundry room window and lapped, her metal collar clinking in rhythm against the steel bowl.

Annette peeled off her wet sweater and undershirt and threw them into the dryer. Should she change her leggings too? They were only a little wet. Yes, she decided she would. She pulled them off with her socks in tow, threw them all in and turned on the dryer. She didn't wait to hear if the dryer started up, just turned on her heel and walked out of the room. She padded quickly up the carpeted stairs in her underwear to the master bedroom and put on a clean, long sleeved undershirt, fresh socks, and dry leggings. Still sweaty from the brisk hike they'd had, she didn't bother layering with a second top.

She stuck her head into the office where her husband Marcel was working at his desk and asked, "I'm having a yoghurt and granola, would you like some?"

Marcel looked up at her, thought for a moment and replied, "I think I'll pass. I'll make something a little later." It hadn't been that long since the breakfast he had eaten when Annette left at 8am for her morning walk with the dogs. He added, "By the way, the power's out again." This was happening a lot lately, but it wasn't usually out for more than an hour.

"Oh! I guess the dryers not working then? Hopefully it'll be back on tonight so I can dry my stuff for tomorrow," Annette commented.

Their home was nestled in a quiet residential neighbourhood of Coquitlam, BC, the kind with safe streets and schools nearby, and a creek running through their back yard. It was possible the heavy rains had caused trees to topple onto power lines nearby, or perhaps there was construction somewhere which was causing power interruptions. Whatever the reason, they knew their power would be restored soon enough.

Once Annette disappeared into the kitchen, he got up to join her. Just because he didn't want to eat didn't mean he didn't want to chat with her while she made hers! After 22 years of marriage she was still his favourite person – best friend, compadre, confidante. Since Annette retired from her job at a major grocery chain two years ago, Marcel had come to cherish the extra time they had together. Her passion for animals had prompted friends to urge her to be a dog walker, a lucrative career, especially on the west coast. Everyone called her a "Dog Whisperer" because of her ability to understand and communicate with dogs.

He sat at the kitchen table while Annette prepared her snack. They sat together and chatted amiably about nothing, as couples do. When her meal was done, Annette rinsed her spoon and put it in the dishwasher, then prepared to leave. After a quick trip to the bathroom, she gathered up her wallet and cell phone. She considered taking her usual hiking supplies – bear bell, whistle, water, granola bar, dog treats, gum, walking stick - but she decided against them. This was just going to be a quick hike because Bubba, the small, black, pudgy Puggle she walked in the afternoons, was 13 years old and tired easily; she wouldn't be needing the extra stuff this time.

Chloe and Roxy watched her closely and immediately stood when they saw her open the hall closet. Before her hand even touched the hanger, the dogs were beside her, eagerly wagging their tails knowing what was about to happen.

Annette decided against wearing a sweatshirt under her coat, but since the forecast called for more rain, she put on a toque and two raincoats. The thin, light, nylon, pink, waist-length one went underneath the longer, navy blue one. The blue one had snaps on the pockets, so it would keep her cell phone somewhat dry if it started to really pour. The pink one had pockets, but they didn't close. The dogs tried to contain their excitement, but Roxy was unable to control herself and did mini leaps with her front paws. Annette laughed and shook her head, "I know girl, we're going now."

She pulled on her Bogs because her hiking boots were still wet from the morning's walk around the upper loop at Burke Mountain. The Bogs had thick soles with good grip for the slippery forest debris of the Northwest. If she had to climb over logs to gather dogs, these mid-calf-high boots were safer.

Marcel gave his wife kisses (always three!) and headed back upstairs to resume work with his cell phone. The power was still out but his cell battery was at 90% - no need to panic quite yet! He stopped on the stairs, looked down to Annette and said, as he always did, "Drive carefully.

Have fun!"

When she opened the garage door, the dogs rushed past Annette and raced to the side of the grey, 2000 Toyota Sienna mini-van. Annette opened the sliding door and held Roxy's collar to give Chloe room to jump in first. Roxy wriggled and whined, anxiously awaiting her turn to hop up. Once inside, both dogs turned and doggy-smiled at her as she closed the side door.

Bubba had an 11:30 pick up time. Annette could hear him barking excitedly as she walked up to the side entrance to the house. Annette punched in the door code, opened the door, and Bubba bounded out, as much as the little dog could bound. Bubba had a large tumor just behind his front, left leg, and while it made him look wider than he really was, it also made him less agile than he once had been. Annette let him into the van by the side door and climbed back into the driver's side, looking forward to being back out in the fresh air of the mountains.

She pulled the van out of the driveway, took a right at Hockaday, a left at Robson, straight across Pinetree Way, then eventually one final right onto Plateau Boulevard. The foursome drove up toward Eagle Mountain along the winding road, wending their way uphill as cul-de-sacs with mid-sized family homes gave way to upscale town homes and then to forest on the left.

On the right, a sprawling golf course ran behind the gated townhome community which lined the street. At the corner past the golf course, a smaller access road headed straight while the main road veered left and back downhill. Here, the golf course jumped the small access road and continued on the other side of Plateau Boulevard. The small bit of access road was the end point on this side of Eagle Mountain.

The heavy, yellow, metal bar which served as a gate at the access road was always unlocked and swung open, so Annette drove the van into the service road. She liked to walk the dogs here, as they weren't as likely to run into other people (or dogs) on these trails.

There were a few other cars in the first small lot, so Annette drove past it and parked her van by the side of the road near the golf course's maintenance yard, as near as she could get to the trail she and the dogs would take. When she opened the side door, the dogs all but flew out, immediately heading for the trail with their noses to the ground. There were so many fresh things to smell as it had been raining almost non-stop since the last time they were here!

Annette tucked some plastic poop bags into her raincoat and closed up the van. She patted the right pocket of her outer raincoat to make sure her phone was there, then dropped the keys into the left, outer pocket so they wouldn't scratch the face of her cell (it was a new phone, so she wanted to treat it with care.) She looked up at the heavy dark clouds with a sigh as she adjusted her toque and pulled on her thin, grey gloves, then headed up the road after the dogs. Even if the rain came, it never stopped her from taking the dogs out.

Monday, November 20th, 1:00pm

The dogs criss-crossed over the trail, alternately running up ahead or waiting for Annette to catch up, leaping over logs and snuffling bushes on both sides of the path. Chloe chased birds and squirrels, barking as she challenged their right to be there. Roxy didn't wander off as far as Chloe but was equally eager to chase critters. Bubba waddled along happily, small but tough in his own right. There was no need for a leash here in the forest because the dogs always came when she called.

They trudged along what looked like an old logging road, probably used a hundred years ago to log the old cedars. The massive, eight-foot-high stumps with notches from logging planks were the only vestiges of what once was a magnificent forest of giants, and the logging trail was evidence of their demise. Progress had its price, but the forest had been making its comeback all along. It was now a protected forest within the Coquitlam watershed and was safe from logging. Aside from the occasional removal of windthrow or diseased trees, the ecosystem was untouched by machinery. Though outdoor enthusiasts with mountain bikes had ripped up the forest floor near the road, the downed trees prohibited the access of even the most adaptive vehicles further in from the forest's edge.

The rutted trail was full of water thanks to a month's worth of heavy rainfall and the dogs stopped occasionally to have a drink in the puddles. Annette hopped across the path at a dry spot and took a trail which would lead her south toward the powerline. She gave a "whoop-whoop" so the dogs would know to follow her. Sometimes she called who-who or woohoo or wup wup, but whatever she said, the dogs knew the tone in her voice and came running.

As they neared the edge of the bush where sunlight reached the forest floor and allowed plants to thrive, the undergrowth was thicker so they all stuck to the small deer trail instead of bushwhacking. When they came out into the pipeline clearing, which ran parallel to the powerline but was narrower, the dogs gave themselves a shake to clear their fur. Annette took off her toque and brushed off some twigs and leaves which had fallen on her during their trek through the heavier brush, then pulled it back on and headed east along the cleared path. They walked parallel to the powerline access road but stayed on the pipeline clearing to avoid any vehicle encounters. It was rare to see anyone driving down the access road but just in case, it was safer to walk the pipeline clearing in case the dogs zigged when they should've zagged. The two roads met in a large cleared area where the powerlines veered to the right and the pipeline clearing forged straight ahead.

The foursome circled the metal fence protecting the compressor station and continued along the pipeline clearing for about 50 feet. Up ahead Annette could see a metal fence blocking the path, so she re-entered the forest along a small trail to her left. The dogs raced ahead. Annette pulled out her phone to check the time. It was almost 2:00pm already – they had been hiking for nearly two hours. Time whizzed by when everyone was enjoying the break in the weather!

As Annette walked she heard her phone buzz. It was a text message from Marcel: *Still no power here.*

Annette dictated to her phone using the voice-to-text option: *That's too bad. It's getting a little too much with the power being out, that's four times in the last three weeks.*

There must be a number to call BC Hydro and find out when the power is going to come back on, she spoke into the phone.

Marcel: *Yeah, I will try to find that.*

A few minutes later Annette got another text from Marcel: *Uggg… estimate is 4:00!*

Annette: *Well that's the shits. What are you going to do?*

Marcel: *Go shopping I guess.*

They hadn't had time to do their usual grocery run on the weekend, so with the power out and the laptop batteries almost exhausted, he figured he would take advantage of the downtime.

Marcel: *Gabrielle is on her way home… English was canceled.*

Annette and Marcel's daughter, Gabrielle studied at Langara College and still lived at home to cut costs. In order to save her money and time, they would often pick her up from the nearest Skytrain station and bring her home.

Annette: *What time will she be at the Evergreen station? Did you want me to pick her up?*

Marcel: *She is just leaving, so shortly after 3. I can get her.*

There was nothing pressing at home, so he would be happy to have an excuse to leave and pick up their daughter. There was currently a nice break in the weather and Annette would probably like to take full advantage of that with the dogs.

There was a Costco not too far from the train station, so Marcel grabbed his keys and headed out a little early. He picked up a pre-cooked chicken for the family's dinner that night and a nice roast beef to cook for the next night. As he was leaving the store, he caught a whiff of their delicious hotdogs and caved to the temptation. The $1.50 deal even included a drink – it was a no-brainer! Hunger satiated, he picked up Gabrielle at 3:15 and the two headed for home to see if the power was back on.

Annette's phone rang. She unsnapped her pocket again, pulled out the phone and looked at the display. It was her friend Nadine calling. She would call Annette every day in the early afternoon to chat when she was driving home from work. The timing often coincided with Annette's afternoon walk with the dogs. Annette enjoyed the distant camaraderie and Nadine enjoyed the company on her drive home from work. The friends could catch up while still keeping an eye on the dogs and the road, respectively. It was a win-win. The friends chatted at length about the previous Sunday's Christmas party they had attended with girlfriends, gushing about what a good time they'd had.

Their phone calls always included Nadine asking Annette how many dogs she had, where they were, and where they were going. But today, before that familiar conversation came up, Roxy the boxer began to bark. Roxy often barked at the wildlife, but it was usually brief, just enough to give the animal a fair warning. This time she barked on and on, so there must've been something other than a bird catching her attention.

Nadine could hear the barking so asked, "Who's doing all the barking?"

"That's Roxy," Annette told her. "I'd better go see what she's up to. I'll call you back." She hung up and put her phone back into her pocket, then picked up the pace to catch up to Roxy.

Annette looked up from the trail to see a figure approaching on the next trail, about 30 feet to her right. He was a younger man, someone she had seen before on the Eagle Mountain trails. She always made an effort to be friendly, with a "hello" or "they don't bite" or whatever, but she never received a response. He never spoke to her, merely looked past her and continued on his way. She didn't take it personally, as she knew not everyone was chatty or friendly, especially when they were in the woods taking in nature and enjoying the solitude. But she thought it odd that he wouldn't even acknowledge her with so much as a nod or a smile. As a 4'11", 130lb woman alone on a forested trail, she was aware bad things could happen and quiet characters were especially suspicious.

Roxy picked up on Annette's uneasiness and barked at the man again, though she kept her distance and barked from the halfway point between the two trails. Roxy wasn't dangerous in the least, but she was a large dog and some people might be scared of her. She said to the stranger, "I'm really sorry, she just barks, she won't bite," but once again, he carried on walking past without a word or a nod of thanks.

After he passed, Annette let Roxy's collar go and watched her gallop after the other two dogs, who had run up ahead on the trail. It was probably time to head back, but she wanted to give the silent man a few minutes to get well ahead of them first. The dogs were happily exploring and since they weren't in a hurry, she'd let them play a bit longer.

The dogs wandered to the right, off the scant trail. Annette followed, not wanting to lose sight of them before they had to turn around. The dogs leapt easily over downed logs and little creeks, but it was a challenge for Annette to keep up with them. She didn't mind – as long as she could see them, they could wander as they pleased. She walked atop downed logs so she could see further from her perch, and also to avoid the debris on the forest floor - it was often easier to walk on the drying logs than in the slick undergrowth of the damp rainforest.

As Annette balanced along a medium-sized log, she realized it must be about time to be heading back to the van. She turned on her heel mid-log and headed back toward the larger log which was laying perpendicular and would take her back toward the van. After a few steps she decided she should call for the dogs so they would know she had changed course. She spun around to call into the forest and promptly lost her footing.

Annette awoke to a searing pain in her left side. She was laying on the ground on her left side, between the two logs. Had she passed out? How long had she been unconscious? Had she hit her head? Roxy was over her, looking down at her as if seeing if she was okay. Chloe stood a few feet away, also looking at her. Bubba was nowhere in sight.

She tried to sit up but there was a stabbing pain in her left side as soon as she tried to move her legs. Maybe she had landed on a log or a root and it was digging into her. She rolled to her right and onto her stomach to get into a position where she could push herself up onto her knees. She took a deep breath and pushed herself up onto all fours, the pain in her side shooting into her hip and lower back as she rose. She glanced at the ground where she had landed but there was nothing sticking out that she could see. It was a grey day and the fading light was of no help, so it was possible there was a root underneath the leaves.

Annette pulled her right knee under her chest and got her foot under her pelvis to get ready to carry her weight. She pulled her torso up and raised her head to look for Bubba. From her crouch, she could see Roxy and Chloe, but not the short Puggle. She called for him, exacerbating the pain in her side by the effort her lungs made. Bubba didn't come. Annette figured he was off following a scent with that beagle nose of his.

Annette let out a soft sigh and braced herself for the pain she was about to endure by attempting to stand up. There was nothing to grab onto to steady herself, so she placed both hands on her raised right knee and pushed down while pulling her left leg forward and under her. She got up slowly, her worry about the dogs pushing her past the pain in her side but letting out a scream in pain because of it. Once upright, she could see over the surrounding logs. No Bubba in sight.

"Bubba? Bubba," she called into the woods as loudly as she could, but her voice was weak and she couldn't take deep breaths because of the sharp pain in her side. Adrenaline took over and she forced herself to move. She HAD to find Bubba! Unsure of which way to search, she headed for the path of least resistance. The fewer fallen trees she had to climb over, the easier it would be for her to walk as lifting her legs too high caused sharp pains along her left side. Besides, Bubba's legs were only about six inches long – he wasn't likely to go jumping over tall logs!

Without her really noticing, a light drizzle had started, and though her clothing became increasingly wet, Annette continued looking for the missing dog. To her last breath, she would protect the dogs in her charge.

She had proven this earlier in the year when she had fallen into an eddy at the bottom of a waterfall while trying to save one of the dogs in her care who had slipped into the water. The rocks surrounding the waterfall had been worn smooth and were slippery with moss, thwarting her attempts to climb out. By God's grace, two people happened by and came to her aid by forming a human chain to pull Annette and the dog out of the water. She had insisted they take the dog out first and would not even consider leaving the waterfall without the pooch. After many protests, her rescuers could see she would not give in, and they pulled the exhausted and panicked dog out by the collar. Only then did Annette take the outstretched hand and let them pull her out of the water. No, leaving a dog behind was not an option for her.

"Bubba…. Bubba," she called out, hoping he would drop what ever scent he was following and come back to her. "Bubba… where are you?" she said quietly, holding her side, starting to get very concerned. "What a dumb-ass I am," she thought quietly, angry at herself for not being more careful.

Salal bushes pulled at her feet, branches caught her as she stumbled over windthrow, her gloved hands slipped on mossy bark as she steadied herself on tree trunks. The only thing on Annette's mind was finding that dog. She pushed onward, expecting Bubba to come barrelling at them from around the next tree.

Annette instinctively moved downhill. It was the easiest for her, and probably for Bubba too. It took less effort than climbing uphill, though it was the opposite of the direction she needed to go. The van was half way up the mountain, an almost lateral walk from where she was. Besides, the pipeline clearing was this way… wasn't it? Shock was setting in and being cold and wet added to her dazed state of mind. Holding onto the thought of finding Bubba kept her upright and moving but didn't allow for her to be clear-headed about directions.

Sploosh Annette let out a yelp as her foot sunk into a hidden, boggy creek. The water rushed into her boot, soaking her already damp sock. Leggings were proving to be a poor choice for today's adventure. She couldn't pull the boot up without putting the other foot down too, so now she was up to her knees in water. The dogs easily hopped over the bog while Annette clambered out of the muddy soup. Her toes squished in water inside her boot as she walked, but she didn't have the energy or the time to stop, pull her boots off, and pour out the water. She was on a mission to find Bubba and the thin winter light was fading fast.

A short while later, they came upon a small stream she couldn't remember seeing before. On the bank there was an old, rusty pile of metal, probably something left behind when they logged this area over 100 years ago. No, she'd definitely remember seeing that, even if she didn't remember the stream. Laying across the stream was a wide log the threesome could use to go across. Annette climbed on top of the log with some effort and looked back, expecting both dogs to follow. Instead, they stood on the riverbank looking up at her, watching her. "Come on," she encouraged them. They stood their ground. Annette crouched down, sat on the log, then slid herself back to the ground, trying to move as gently as possible. The muscles in her side and back were seizing up, making her movements stiffer by the minute.

After multiple attempts to convince Roxy to climb up onto the makeshift bridge, Annette gave up. As she led the dogs back in the direction they had come from, she realized it was unlikely Bubba would've taken it upon himself to cross that stream. It didn't make any sense, but then again, not much was making sense right now. Her brain was fighting to stay present, but it was getting more difficult by the minute to stay alert.

It was getting late. Sunset came around 4:30 these days, but the tall trees and long shadows made darkness come even faster in the forest. She had to call Marcel and ask him to come help look for Bubba. He could bring her whistle, surely Bubba would hear it! Dry socks would be a bonus too.

She reached for the raincoat's right pocket and found it unsnapped. And empty! Her phone was missing! It must have fallen out of her pocket when she took that tumble. "Oh NO!" she thought, more worried about Marcel's reaction to losing the phone than about her current situation. That phone had belonged to a dear friend who had passed away recently, and his widow had sold it to Marcel. It was a special phone and Marcel was going to be annoyed if she had lost it for good. "Damn it!" she spat, mentally kicking herself for having dropped the cellphone. She would look for it after she found Bubba.

But where did she fall? She had walked so far through the bush now, she couldn't backtrack to find her phone. Everything looked the same. Did she come from that direction? Or THAT direction? That tree looked familiar, but so did that one. Which way was it to the path? To the parking lot?

It didn't matter. Annette could either go looking for the phone or go looking for the dog. Her first choice would always be the dogs. Always. Phones could be replaced. She renewed her resolve to find Bubba.

Monday, November 20th, 4:00pm

The power had still not come back on when Gabrielle and Marcel got home, but by 4:00pm the clock on the microwave started flashing. Gabrielle was working on an assignment and since dinner was already taken care of, Marcel offered to help. They sat together in the office and discussed the essay she was writing for English. It was a difficult subject to write on, so she was having troubles finding resource material. Marcel tried to guide her on how to find sources instead of outright giving them to her, so he was supportive but not overbearing. It was a fine balance he'd learned from years of helping with elementary and high school homework.

At 4:30, Marcel looked out the window and noticed daylight was starting to fade. He wasn't concerned about Annette, but he wanted to know what time she would be home so he could get dinner on the table. He sent her a text hoping for an eta.

"Hey sweetie, how ya doing?" he tapped into his phone.

There was no immediate reply, and no "writing in progress" dots.

Marcel went back to helping Gabrielle with her paper, thinking Annette was probably gabbing with one of the dog's owners at their door and couldn't hear her phone because she'd left it in the van.

Annette carefully lowered herself down onto a log, trying to pull her raincoat under her bum to avoid getting even more wet. She needed to sit and think for a minute, to get her bearings. Roxy and Chloe came near to see what she was up to, then continued to explore but close by this time. They sensed her worry and stayed at the ready in case their pack leader needed them.

It was dark and getting darker by the minute. There were no street lights for miles, no headlights streaking through the trees. Even her little pen light was hooked onto her other jacket, the one hanging in her closet at home.

"Well guys," Annette said to the dogs, "looks like we're here for the night! We'll have to find Bubba in the morning." She slid down the side of the log to the ground, steadying herself with her hands to lower her body gently. The muscles in her side were definitely seizing up, and she had to put a hand down first in order to lower her bottom onto the ground, her face grimacing in pain as she did so.

Once sitting, she made an attempt to get her boots off and pour out the water. By then her left side was so sore she couldn't pull her knees up let alone get the boots off. Pulling with her arms put too much pressure on her core, pulling at the sore and seized muscles on her back and side. She gave up, pulled up the hood of her raincoat and lay down on her back next to the log. In so much pain, it was impossible to get comfortable and she couldn't even lay on her side like she usually did to fall asleep. The best she could do was lay on her back with her arms across her chest to keep herself warm. But she wasn't warm. She was cold. Cold and soaked through.

Roxy and Chloe circled, then sat nearby staring at her. Roxy whined anxiously, her eyes darting from Annette to Chloe to the forest and back to Annette. "It's okay," Annette told her, trying to soothe herself as much as the dogs. Roxy curled up beside a nearby log and Chloe stayed sitting up, watching Annette closely. Their old border collie Sara would've spooned with her but unfortunately Chloe wasn't the snuggling type. Dogs had certain traits in common within a breed but they certainly had their own personalities.

The only faint light Annette could see came from above the trees, a dim reflection of city lights on the clouds. If she looked with her peripheral vision she could see the outlines of the dogs but little else. Chloe shivered in the cold as she stood guard, Roxy lay on the ground licking herself for comfort. There was nothing more to be done, all they could do was wait for daylight to continue the search for Bubba.

Even though it was dark and she was physically exhausted from struggling with the pain, it was still early in the evening. Annette thought it might be only 5pm, but it felt like midnight. It would be impossible to sleep, with rain falling on her face and thoughts swirling in her head. She worried about the little boy she occasionally drove to school in the morning to help a friend who had to work early some days. Who would take him to school if she wasn't there? Would Marcel know to call the boy's mother so she could make arrangements? Annette loved taking him to school. Spending those precious moments with that sweet boy made her remember when Gabrielle was that small, and though she decided she was too young to be a grandmother, she knew if and when the time came, she'd be a hands-on grandparent. Maybe she'd even get to take her own grandchildren to school.

And what about Roxy's and Bubba's owners? They were going to be so worried about their dogs! Would they think she kidnapped them? Would they be angry with her for keeping them out all night? She hoped they knew she would do her best to get them all out alive. It had been less than four years since a dogwalker from Langley had reported six dogs stolen from her truck when in fact they had died from heat exhaustion after she left them in the hot truck. She had dumped their bodies in a ditch in the neighbouring city of Abbotsford, where they were discovered five days later. Annette's sense of responsibility was such that this sort of behaviour would never enter her mind, but who knew what the owners would think? Hopefully they knew that Annette would put the dogs' health and well-being above hers.

Other dogs were being dropped off in the morning. What would their owners do? She had people who relied on her and she felt horrible for disappointing them!

How about Marcel? Surely, he would have noticed her absence by now? Was he out looking for her? He was going to give her hell for not taking her gear with her when she left the house! If she'd had her whistle, she could've called for Bubba or maybe someone in the forest would've heard her and come to help.

Annette twisted her wedding ring and began to cry. There was no point wiping away tears as they just mingled with the rain falling on her face. She wished she could close her eyes and wake up in her own bed, having had a terrible dream instead of living this nightmare.

How did this happen? How did she end up here? Where did she go wrong? She felt like the last person on earth, so alone, so isolated. And thirsty. She hadn't eaten since before noon but she was not hungry at all, only thirsty.

Annette let out a heavy sigh and tried to close her eyes. She listened in the darkness. It was true what people said: silence was deafening! Aside from the hiss of the rain, the only other sounds were Roxy's nervous licking and her own teeth chattering from the cold. And yet, her eardrums were humming with a white noise. She gave her head a small shake hoping to clear her mind, but the silence filled her head so much she couldn't concentrate enough to allow her thoughts to drown it out. She faded in and out of consciousness, thinking only three things:

Stay alive. Find Bubba. Get out.

Stay alive. Find Bubba. Get out.

Stay alive. Find Bubba. Get out.

Roxy's growl brought her to wakefulness just as she was about to nod off. Her ears strained to hear something, anything. Nothing. The ground was hard and dug into her shoulder blades. She tried to adjust her position but it was no use. There was no soft place to lay, and if she moved too much the pain in her side made her breath catch. She pulled the raincoat's hood over her ears to keep the rain out of her face a bit better. She finally allowed exhaustion to overtake her.

When Annette hadn't replied by 5:30, Marcel sent her another text.

"Hhhhheeeellllllllooooooooooooo" to which there was no reply.

Five long minutes ticked by, and now a niggling feeling was growing inside his gut.

Marcel called Annette's phone. It rang the requisite four times before going to voicemail. He waited a few seconds and tried again. Ringing. Voicemail. Again. Ringing. Voicemail. The only thing he could conclude is the phone was definitely ringing, Annette just couldn't hear it. If the battery had died or the phone was turned off or out of range, it would've gone immediately to voicemail and it wouldn't ring on his end at all!

With growing concern, Marcel used his laptop to sign into Annette's iCloud account to do a "find my phone" search. Her phone could not be located. What was going on??

Marcel phoned Roxy's owner to ask if the dog had returned home yet. Roxy's owner didn't answer the call. Next he phoned Bubba's owner, Tina, to ask if Bubba had been brought back.

"Hello," Tina answered

"Hi Tina, this is Marcel. Hey, has Annette dropped Bubba off yet?"

"I don't know, I'm not home yet. Why, is there something wrong?" Concern crept into her voice.

"I don't know yet. It's dark out and she hasn't come home yet. Just wanted to know if she was at your place. She may have gone to do something after dropping the dogs off," he replied.

"Well, I am on the North Shore right now, on my way home. I can call you back in an hour and let you know if Bubba's home," Tina said.

"Thanks Tina. I will let you know if I hear from her," Marcel said, then hung up.

It was now quarter to six at night. The sun had long since set and the darkness made the situation more ominous. Marcel had to go out and look for her.

"Something's not right here," he told Gabrielle, "I can't just sit here. I'm going to see if I can find her. I'll be in touch, let me know right away if you hear from her." He grabbed his jacket and headed out to the garage with his wallet, phone, and car keys.

As he put the keys in the ignition, he thought about where he would check first. Recently Annette had been frequenting Burke Mountain, so that was a good place to start. It was nearby and only took 10 minutes to drive to where she usually parked at the trailhead.

He arrived to find the spot dark and empty. This was a relief and gave him hope Annette was simply visiting with friends.

Marcel called his daughter to let her know what he had found, or rather, hadn't found, and let her know where he would check next.

Ten minutes later he showed up at Janet's house, Roxy's home. There were no lights on, at least none that he could see, but Marcel knocked on the door anyway. He waited a few seconds but impatience came over him and he got back in the car to check elsewhere.

At about 6:15, he pulled up to Annette's friend Sandy's house. He didn't see Annette's van. Disappointed and worried, he got back into his car just as his phone rang. Praying it was Annette as he looked at the call display, he was slightly disappointed to see that it was Janet returning his call.

"Hi Janet" he said, hoping she would say Roxy was home.

"Marcel, sorry, I couldn't get back to you right away, I was working a bit late. Wayne has been trying to contact Annette because he is supposed to pick Roxy up today. Are they home?" she asked. Wayne was her husband who often picked up Roxy.

"No, not yet. I was hoping you saw her. I'm starting to get pretty worried," Marcel confided in Janet.

"She's not home yet? Where could she be?" said Janet, matching his worry.

"I don't know. I'm in the car now, looking for her. I drove up to Burke Mountain but she wasn't there. I drove by your house, and just left her friend Sandy's house. No sign of her. I'm going to look up at Eagle Mountain. I sure hope she isn't there!" Marcel exclaimed.

"Oh my god Marcel, she better just be getting groceries or something," Janet blurted.

"I hope so. If you see or hear from her, have her call me right away. I'll let you know if I hear from her," he promised.

"Ok Marcel, I hope you find her. Good luck!" Janet said and disconnected.

Where could they be? It wasn't like Annette to be so late and not let him know, and it was certainly out of character for her to not have the dogs back before dark!

If Annette hadn't taken the dogs to Burke Mountain, there were only two other places she would go. Marcel decided to check Eagle Mountain first. At 6:35 he drove up the access road and turned the corner to the lot where he knew Annette usually parked. It was pitch black on the mountain, the darkness of the trees making the forest look more sinister than in daylight. As his headlights swung around the bend, they reflected off the tail lights of a vehicle. Annette's van!

Marcel's heart sank. Something was wrong. Very wrong. He immediately called Gabrielle to let her know where he was and what he'd found. He said he'd call her back in a bit, he wanted to check the van. He pointed his car at the van and left his headlights on so he could see through the dark.

He got out of his car and walked past the van to the locked gate blocking the end of the access road. He whistled and yelled, hoping at least the dogs would respond to his calls. Silence. He walked to the van and circled around to the driver's side door. He tried the door. Locked. He cupped his hands to the window to peer inside. Empty.

He turned back to the gate, thinking he would go in and find her himself. He quickly realized how hopeless that was in the pitch dark. He wouldn't even be able to see the gate if it wasn't for the headlights on the car. He needed help. He needed to talk to Gabrielle. He needed Annette…

Marcel phoned Gabrielle and told her, "Hi, Sweetie, I found Mom's van!"

"Where is it," Gabrielle asked.

"It's up on Eagle Mountain. I'm so sorry, Sweetie, it looks like she is still out there!"

"Oh no," Gabrielle said softly.

"I know, hopefully she isn't too far away. I can't stay on the line, I need to call 911. I need help up here," Marcel said, trying to sound confident.

"Ok, Dad. I love you," she said and hung up.

Marcel called 911 at 6:40pm.

"Police, Ambulance or Fire?" the calm woman's voice asked.

"Um... Search and Rescue?" he replied, not knowing who he was supposed to ask for help.

Seconds later, Marcel heard, "RCMP, what's your emergency?"

"Hi, I just found my wife's van up on Eagle Mountain. She was out hiking today and didn't come back. I think she's lost out in the woods," Marcel heard himself say. He couldn't believe he was saying these words.

"I understand your wife is lost in the woods. Do you know for sure she is in there?" the operator responded.

"Yes, she's a dog walker. She didn't come home before it got dark. I was worried, so I went to the places she normally parks and found her van on Eagle Mountain," Marcel said, his voice starting to get shaky with urgency.

"Can you tell me where you are right now?" she asked.

"I am up at the Westwood Plateau Golf and Country Club maintenance yard," Marcel answered.

"Thank you, sir. I have dispatched a car up there, it should be there in a few minutes. Does your wife have a mobile phone?" the operator asked.

"Yes, she does."

"Can you give me her phone number?" Marcel responded with her number and the woman said, "I know it's hard, but please don't call or text her anymore. We need to conserve her battery in case we have any chance of locating her with that. Also, please do not go anywhere near her vehicle. I have dispatched a dog team and they will try to get her scent."

"I have been calling and the call doesn't go directly to her voice mail, so I am pretty sure it is receiving calls," Marcel offered, trying to be helpful.

"Yes, I see that. Please don't call anymore. Can you tell me who Nadine is? She was the last person your wife talked to on her phone," the operator reported.

Marcel was surprised they already had that kind of information from Annette's phone. "That's Annette's friend," he answered as he watched headlights coming up the access road.

The first RCMP officer had arrived and pulled up next to Marcel without exiting his vehicle.

"Can you please get into your car and follow me out of this area?" he asked. Marcel got in his car, turned it around and followed the officer just outside the main gate to Plateau Boulevard. The officer parked his car on the side of the access road and Marcel parked right behind him. They both got out and walked to the sidewalk.

The officer reached his hand out. "Constable Clark," he announced.

"Hi. Marcel. Good to see you here," Marcel introduced himself.

"Can you tell me what happened?" the officer asked. Marcel explained how Annette wasn't home before dark and where he went looking her. As he spoke, a police SUV raced through the gate and up the access road. Coquitlam RCMP Dog Team was written on the back of the vehicle. It was followed by another RCMP car.

"A dog team is there now trying to get the scent. Can you tell me exactly where you walked up there?" Constable Clark asked.

"I walked to the van, tried to open the driver's side door, then walked up the access road to the next gate that is closed. I stood there for a bit, then walked back down to my car where I phoned 911," Marcel described.

"Ok. It's been raining off and on today, but they will do their best to try to find her track," the Constable said as two more police cars raced up the street.

As the two talked about what was taking place, Marcel's phone rang. The call display showed Nadine, so he excused himself from the officer and answered.

"Marcel, what's going on? What's happened to Annette?" she asked worriedly.

"I don't know yet. She didn't come home, so I went looking for her and found her van on the plateau," Marcel told her.

"Oh my God, Marcel. That girl…" she began, leaving the rest unsaid. Annette was known for being the adventurous one, always up for doing something out of the ordinary. "I got a call from the police wanting to know about our last conversation. I told them how it was common that we chat in the afternoons and that we ended the call with Roxy barking," Nadine said.

"Wow, they sure got a hold of you quickly," Marcel marvelled. "They have her number and are trying to track her phone down with that, so don't call it. They need to conserve the batteries."

"I don't know what to do Marcel. How can I help?" she asked in dismay.

Marcel knew what he need from her. "Could you please go down to be with Gabrielle? She is alone right now and needs somebody to be with. That would be a huge help for me," Marcel suggested, always thinking about others.

"Ok, Breanne and I will go right down. I'm also going to call Sascha to be with you. I think you need help too," she said. Nadine's daughter Breanne and Gabrielle were close friends and Nadine looked at Gabrielle as a second daughter. They were the perfect people to take care of Gabrielle in an emergency. Sascha was a mutual friend, part of the close friends who always did things together.

"Thank you, Nadine. I appreciate it," Marcel said, starting to get emotional.

"Don't worry, honey," Nadine reassured him. "They'll find her."

Marcel called Gabrielle again to give her an update.

"The police are here now and have dog teams looking for her. It's all happening really fast. I don't know too much yet. I just talked to Nadine, she and Breanne are on their way to the house to be with you. I don't want you to be alone right now," he said.

"Thank you, Dad. I love you!"

"I love you too, sweetheart," Marcel echoed, wishing he could be there with her but knowing he had to stay put.

Marcel hung up and walked back to the officer to see if there were any developments.

"We have two police dogs in there right now trying to pick up a scent. They aren't equipped for a forest search, so they are focusing on the golf course fairways and the bush immediately beside them," he explained. "They usually search for about an hour before they will call in Search and Rescue."

Relieved that finally there was action, Marcel took a bit of comfort knowing he wasn't the only one looking for Annette anymore. He was grateful to share the worry with people who knew what to do. They continued some small talk, but for the most part they were silent as they waited for results of the search.

Monday, November 20th, 7:00pm

Shortly after 7:00pm, Marcel's good friends Buffy and Sascha showed up. Sascha and Marcel had been great friends for over 20 years, so it was a big relief to see them. They parked their car down the road a bit, then got out and walked towards Marcel with flashlights in hand. They were both dressed in heavy jackets, obviously ready to head up into the mountains to start the search.

"Hey! How ya doing?" Buffy said, giving Marcel a big hug as they reached him on the sidewalk. Sascha gave him a hug too.

"I've had better days," Marcel replied.

"Yeah, I bet, Nadine called and told us Annette was lost. What happened?" she asked. Marcel went through the story once again, telling them everything that had happened since he started the search. The RCMP officer was also standing nearby listening, trying to hear if there were any extra details. Buffy and Sascha introduced themselves to the officer.

"Um, I see that you both have flashlights," the officer said gingerly to them. "You know you won't be going out there looking for them. One missing person is enough for one night," he said with a smile.

Buffy and Sascha looked at the flashlights in their hands and snickered. "Yeah, I guess that wouldn't be a good idea. We just didn't know what to expect," Sascha said. As much as the pair had wanted to race into the dark forest and start yelling for Annette, in a small way they were relieved to be told no. Perhaps they'd be allowed to join the search at daylight.

They stood for the most part in cold, but otherwise comfortable silence. Trying to lighten the mood a bit, Marcel said, "I keep expecting to see her walking down the road with the dogs. She lost track of time and had to take a different exit from the mountain and is just walking down the road to get her van."

"Yeah, I can just hear her now," Buffy said, "'What are you dumb asses doing here? Why didn't you come get me?'" trying to sound like Annette. They had a giggle at that, but the merriment didn't last long.

Marcel strained his eyes into the darkness, hoping to find shadows emerging into the streetlights. As he peered up the Parkway Boulevard, the road that jutted uphill to the left then followed the golf course back down the hill, his eyes caught a glimpse of someone watching them from the upstairs window of an adjacent townhouse. They stood in a dark room looking down at them through a window. What must they be thinking? "Do they think we are criminals being apprehended by RCMP?" Marcel wondered. Or were they familiar with this scene, having witnessed it when others hadn't arrived back from their forest wanders?

There was very little to say to anyone, but it was comforting to have people around him. Marcel was thankful they didn't ply him with too many questions or try to take his mind off it. That would only have agitated him. Any small talk was brief and quiet, mere murmurs in the night.

The first Search and Rescue volunteer showed up around 7:45pm in a small car. He parked nearby and walked over to talk with the officer, then returned to his car. The RCMP must have called in the Search and Rescue people without Marcel's knowledge, not wanting or needing to waste time filling him in on their every move.

Shortly after that, the SAR Mobile Command Centre vehicle came around the corner and headed down Plateau Boulevard, the car with the first SAR member following. The officer walked over to Marcel and informed him they had decided to set up base at the Hampton Park Elementary School down the road. They didn't want anyone up the access road to try to preserve the scene. He asked Marcel and his friends to follow him to the school.

Buffy got in the car with Marcel, and Sascha got into his own car to follow the RCMP officer to the parking lot of the school. They drove a few blocks down Plateau Boulevard and turned right onto Paddock Drive. Half a block later they came upon the school on the right-hand side.

Once in the parking lot, they all got out of their cars and stood in front of the command centre vehicle. The small group hunched their shoulders against the cold and stuffed their hands in their pockets to stave off the night air. They watched in silence as Search and Rescue volunteers arrived in their personal cars and unloaded their gear from their trunks. Waterproof boots, headlamps, rain gear, high visibility vests, and all the necessary gear they would need. They all came prepared to enter the forest to search for his wife. Unpaid and unsung, Marcel admired their dedication and bravery. It took a certain kind of spirit to willingly put oneself in danger to save others.

A truck pulling a trailer containing what looked like an ATV pulled into the lot and parked further down the lot. It would need plenty of room to unload its cargo. The driver unhitched the tailgate and dropped it, then released the straps expertly and efficiently, not wasting a movement. He climbed into the vehicle, started it, and backed it out of the trailer with ease. This was no typical ATV! This was something Marcel had never seen before. It had the body of a jeep but instead of tires it had four triangular tracks like those of a snowcat or snowmobile, the narrow front end containing a winch and probably other gear not readily seen. It reminded him of a vehicle from a James Bond movie, which lent it confidence and a cool factor of 10.

"I'd love to take that thing up the mountain! Annette's limo out of there," Marcel joked to Sascha. The two chuckled and Sascha nodded in agreement. They were unlikely to ever get a chance to ride in that machine, but it was good to see it in action from close up.

A van slowly drove down the street and rolled into the parking lot. It was a media van from a local affiliate of a national broadcaster, the first sign that Annette's disappearance was news. The camera man got busy setting up his gear while the reporter readied his mike and ear piece. It seemed they had respect for his obvious worry and perhaps they could tell from his pacing that his mind was on other things.

SAR member Michael Coyle invited Marcel into the command centre vehicle to show him what was being done. This was likely routine to help distraught family members feel like they were being taken seriously and everything possible was being done to help in the search for the missing. Against one wall were three computer stations with chairs and the opposite wall contained drawers of equipment and a double, sliding whiteboard with a cork board behind it. At the back end there was an ante-room, where there was a bench seat on one wall and two smaller seats with a fold-out table between them on the other wall. It gave Marcel great comfort seeing the professional setting of maps and plotters and all the purposeful activity inside the large vehicle.

"Can you tell us what she was wearing when she left the house today?" asked another SAR member as they stood by the entrance.

Marcel thought for a moment. Though he had kissed her goodbye, he hadn't taken note of what she was wearing. While he was detail oriented for work, clothing was not his forte.

"I don't know what she was wearing underneath, but I know she was wearing her pink and blue raincoat," he offered. "She typically wears that when she thinks it might rain. I know when she got back from her first walk this morning she said her hiking boots were wet, so I'm pretty sure she wore her Bogs," he said as he took out his phone to find a picture of them online.

"Okay, that helps," said the man as he quickly wrote down what Marcel said. "Do you know if she had any gear with her?" he asked hopefully.

Marcel shook his head. "She usually has a day pack with her, but I don't know if she took it. If she did, she'll have bear bells, water, snacks, a whistle, and some other stuff..." his voice trailed off as he realized he didn't know if she'd taken it with her or not, and if she had, why couldn't they hear her whistling?

"Right. So, let's assume she doesn't have that stuff with her. Can you tell me about the dogs she took today? Breed, age, and whatever else you can tell me," the man asked as he looked up at Marcel, his pen poised over his notebook.

Marcel thought carefully, then listed the dogs. "She had our dog Chloe, she's a 6-year-old border collie. She had Roxy, a 3-year-old boxer, and she had Bubba, who's a 13-year-old puggle. He's pudgy and has short legs but the other two are athletic." He sighed. He knew even with short legs, they could have wandered well into the forest in the hours they'd been gone.

Marcel found pictures of the dogs from Annette's Facebook page using a computer in the command truck. She took pictures of the dogs and posted them every day, so it wasn't difficult to find the three together. One of the members quickly printed it on their printer to send out with the search teams. They also posted a picture on the cork board, starting to put their puzzle together.

"One more thing," said the man with the notebook, "are the dogs likely to stay with Annette?"

Without hesitation, Marcel replied an emphatic, "Yes!" There was no question their own dog Chloe would not leave Annette's side, and Roxy was also not one to stray too far away. He wasn't as sure of Bubba, but he was certain at least two of the three would stick close to her.

Once Marcel told them everything he was able to, he joined Buffy and Sascha in the small room at the back of the command truck where they had been invited to wait. There wasn't a lot to watch outside so the friends sat in silence. Searchers had come in individually, assigned to small teams, then ferried up to where Annette's van was parked to start searching their designated areas. The command team members had their heads down, each working on their assigned task, familiarizing themselves with the information Marcel had given them as well as the area maps to try to determine where best to search for quick results.

It was after 9:00pm and the parking lot's lamp posts cast a bright light, but Marcel knew it was pitch black beyond the lighted circle. Marcel excused himself and went to his car, got in, and took out his phone. He opened the Facebook app and started a new post. He wrote:

"Please say a prayer for Annette who is lost up on eagle mtn. Search and rescue is searching... my phone is at 1%... I will update when I can."

He hit the POST button and his phone's battery died. He tried not to take it personally, the battery adding insult to injury in this hour of despair.

Tap tap An RCMP officer tapped at his window. Marcel's heart leapt and he scrambled out of the car. Perhaps there was news? No, there was no news. The officer simply wanted to know if there was a spare set of keys for the van. They wanted to look inside to see if there were any clues to her disappearance.

"Yes, I have a spare set in the garage at home, on the key hooks," Marcel replied.

"I'll go get them," offered Sascha, already with his own keys in his hand. He was eager to help but there wasn't much he and Buffy could do there. Sascha would feel more productive if he could complete a task, no matter how small. Marcel told him exactly where to find the van's spare keys.

"Thanks, Sascha. And could you bring back the charger cable for my phone? It's in the kitchen," Marcel added.

While Sascha retrieved the keys, the RCMP officer asked Marcel questions similar to those already asked by the SAR but for different reasons. Both factions likely needed the details for their reports, but Marcel got the feeling the RCMP were reading more into the answers than the Search and Rescue folks. Were they trying to establish if Marcel was lying? Were they hoping to trip him up? Catch him in a lie? A wavering story? Marcel answered all of his questions with as much honesty as he could – there was no need to tiptoe around any perceived misinformation. He had nothing to hide and knew answering questions honestly was the best policy.

Sasha returned 20 minutes later with the keys, Marcel's phone charger, and a bag of oranges. Gabrielle had sent the oranges. She knew her father hadn't eaten dinner, so she grabbed the first available portable food item she found. Marcel took the bag of oranges but didn't open it. He wasn't hungry, he couldn't have eaten even if he was. Worry had his stomach in knots and food was the furthest thing from his mind.

They returned to the room in the back of the command vehicle, which Marcel had coined 'the anteroom.' He left the oranges on the counter and plugged his phone into a power receptacle beside the table. As they chatted, Bubba's owner Tina pulled up and took two boxes out of the passenger's side of the car. Marcel got up and went outside to greet her.

Tina walked over to Marcel. "Any word?" she asked hopefully, giving Marcel a hug. Marcel shook his head. "I went by the house after I got home and learned you were up here from Nadine," she explained.

"Thanks for coming Tina, I'm glad you're here," Marcel said.

"Once I learned what was happening, I couldn't stay away. If she's out there because of Bubba, I will be very angry at her," she snapped, her worry presenting as anger. If she was worried about Bubba, she was keeping it to herself. She could see Marcel was in no shape to be worrying about dogs when the love of his life was missing.

"I brought coffee for everyone," she said as she held up the two Tim Horton's boxes.

It was as if Mike had super hearing because he immediately poked his head out of the SAR truck and said, "How nice! You can set them up in here," pointing to a table folded out from the side of the command truck. "There's also water and granola bars, help yourselves," Mike offered kindly.

They all returned to the small room in the back of the truck, separated from the command centre by a pocket door. Mike gestured for them to take a seat, and they did so gratefully. Mike left the room, pulling the door closed behind him so they could all have some privacy. The four sat at the table and visibly relaxed in the warmth. Even though it wasn't raining at that point, it was a chilly night and they were all feeling the cold. Nobody took any coffee, but Buffy had put some bottled water on the table and they took them, more for something to hold than to drink. They all stared out the window above the table looking out into the eerie lights of the parking lot.

On the table sat a phone system with a radio speaker, and between their conversations in the truck they could hear the chatter of the search teams in the field. Whenever the speaker chirped, their conversation would stop and the four would stare at the phone with anticipation.

"I see a light," came a static-y voice across the speaker. Marcel and his friends gaped at the speaker and held their breath.

"All search teams turn off your lights," commanded the team leader. "Do you still see the light?" he asked.

"No, it went out," was the reply. Everyone's shoulders sagged, their hopes dashed.

"I need to get some air," said Marcel, excusing himself abruptly and taking his phone off the charger. While he did need to move around a bit, he also needed to urinate in the worst way. He couldn't remember when he'd last emptied his bladder, but he knew he'd been holding it in for the past few hours. He couldn't contain it any longer!

Marcel wandered off, acting as if he was looking at his phone absentmindedly. He opened his Facebook app and read the dozen or so comments which had been written in reply to his last post. He tried to walk to the back of the school inconspicuously and hoped no one would follow him. His taking a pee was neither press-worthy nor of police importance! Once out of sight, he hurriedly put his phone away and did his business behind the nearest bush. That completed, Marcel headed back to the SAR truck. As he rounded the corner to the parking lot, there was the school's custodian offering tea and washrooms to everyone. Huh. Timing really is everything. Under different circumstances, he would've had a good chuckle about that. He shook his head at the display of Murphy's Law and continued to the command centre.

As he walked back into their little room, Marcel's friends looked up at him expectantly. Marcel sank into the bench and hung his head. No news. What was that saying? No news is good news? Well, maybe not in this particular case.

Seeing the pain in Marcel's eyes, Sascha reached across the table and grabbed his arm. "They're going to find her. She's going to be okay," he assured Marcel. Marcel didn't look up but gave a weak smile and nodded. He wavered from being strong to being desperate, and it was starting to show.

The pocket door opened and Mike stood in the doorway. "Can you tell me if Annette had a water bottle with her?" he asked.

"I'm not sure," Marcel answered, "but if she did, it would be a Costco bottle like that one," and he pointed to a Costco bottle Buffy had taken from the SAR supply table.

"Ok. That's not what they found out there," he said with disappointment. Mike started to turn away, then turned back, considering what he wanted to say. "It's not really my place to give advice on what you should do, but I noticed there is media out there. The RCMP might tell you to not talk to them or let them be your spokesperson, but you might want to talk to them. I find the more information they get the better the leads we might get from the public."

"Ok, I'll go chat with them when I can," Marcel said. He had done a few 'guy on the street' type of interviews before, but nothing with this type of situation. He wasn't sure how to approach them or what to say, so wasn't anxious to run right out there.

Before Mike left the room again, there was a chirp from the speaker and Mike noticed the radio on the table. He reached over and turned it off, then unplugged it for good measure. "You might not want to listen to that, there will be a lot of chatter and false positives. It will just get your hopes up. Don't worry, we will let you know if anything happens." Everyone agreed that was best, not having thought of that aspect before.

It was almost 11pm and the one camera crew that was there looked like they were packing up. If Marcel was going to say anything to the media, now was the time to do it. "Might as well get this over with," he whispered to himself as he walked over to them.

"Hi, my name is Marcel, I'm the husband of the lady who is lost," he said as he walked up to them.

"Oh, hi! We were hoping you might come out," the reporter said as the camera man quickly worked to set his camera and lighting back up. Once they were ready with the lights on, the reporter held his microphone out to him. "Could you please tell me your name and spell it out for me?" he asked.

"Sure. Marcel Poitras, M-a-r-c-e-l P-o-i-t-r-a-s." He guessed they liked to make sure they got the captions right when they report the story on the news.

"Can you tell me what happened tonight?" he asked. Marcel described how Annette didn't show up at home when she should have and how he eventually found her van and called 911.

"How's the search going? Any sign of her?"

"No. No sign. They have been searching for a couple of hours and haven't found anything yet," he said, his voice starting to break, thinking of her out there in the cold, dark night. "I'm sorry," he struggled to say as the emotions overtook him. Marcel walked off, trying to collect himself as the reporter and camera man watched. To their credit, they let him go, understanding the struggle he was having. They would have more chances to talk later.

After Marcel took some time to collect himself, he rejoined his friends back in the truck's anteroom. He took a sip of water and sighed. He was tired and emotional, and getting more so with each passing hour. He needed to talk but he was at a loss for words. His friends wanted to comfort him but what could they possibly say to him right now? They had already discussed and re-discussed it from every angle.

Frustrated at his inability to do or say anything productive, Marcel reached for the radio phone on the table that the SAR manager had unplugged and plugged it back in. He snapped it on, wanting to hear anything just to keep himself from thinking bad thoughts. There wasn't much traffic on the radio, and everything that was said was very professional. No words were minced, no elaborations were made. Concise and brief made less margin for errors.

In need of further distractions, Marcel took out his cellphone and checked his Facebook again. A few more messages had come in, but most people were asleep by now and wouldn't see the post until the morning. Marcel's older brother Andy offered to jump into his car and drive down from Kelowna, and while Marcel could use his brother's support, he didn't want him driving for 5 hours in the dark. He messaged back that he would touch bases in the morning. Surely, they would have found her by then.

At 11:55pm, Marcel made the phone call he'd been dreading. He opened his WhatsApp and dialled London, England. He needed to tell Annette's father, Michael and his wife, Deborah about Annette's disappearance. It was just going on 8:00am in London and the two were most likely fixing their morning coffee. They were always happy to hear from Marcel, but this was the hardest conversation they would ever have with him. Marcel gathered his courage and told them everything he knew about the situation, walked them through the search efforts and assured them every effort was being made to bring Annette home safely. It was a very emotional call on both ends of the line. Not a good way to start the morning for them.

As the night wore on, the group of friends went over Nadine's phone call to Annette again and again. Why had Roxy started barking? Was there a bear? A cougar? An attacker? What?? And what about the dogs – if Annette couldn't hear the search teams calling for her, surely the dogs could? And the teams would hear the dogs barking back, wouldn't they?

The entire disappearance was a mystery, and they couldn't fathom what could keep Annette from bringing the dogs back. Simply being lost was probably their best hope because at least then there was a better chance to find them all alive. If they had run into some kind of trouble, the outcome wouldn't be so lucky…

Nobody wanted to think about that.

At around 1am, a female RCMP officer came into the trailer, her dark blue uniform wet and covered with mud up to her thighs. As she grabbed a coffee from one of the Tim Hortons boxes, she told them this was only her second day in the lower mainland, so she was unfamiliar with the terrain. They didn't have forests like this back east! It was quite the job initiation, trudging through the bush in the middle of the night. Marcel gave her a heartfelt, "Thank you for everything you're doing out there."

The search teams started returning to the trailer to take a break and warm up. Mike said, "Marcel, the teams are going to start coming back now. They need to get a bit of food and warm up in the back of the truck. It's stressful out there and they will be joking around a bit, letting off some steam. You might not appreciate their humour right now."

"I completely understand, we will give them their space," Marcel said. He did understand, and he needed people out there who were focused on what they were doing. They needed to have clear heads and not be concerned about what they said around him. Once outside, Mike told Marcel they were focusing their search on the golf course and nearby well-marked trails. It was too dark for the teams to be searching in the off-trail areas, so they would wait for daylight before laying out their routes.

Marcel nodded as Mike spoke, his eyes watching a tall man with a large red beard walking into the trailer. The man looked like he lived in the bush – if anyone could find her that man could, he was sure of it. Marcel's faith in the SAR people was bolstered by seeing the strong and determined faces coming in from the field.

It was late. It had started to rain lightly. Marcel's thin jacket could not protect him from the elements no matter how hard he hunched his shoulders or stomped his feet. He decided he needed to go home. He needed to change his clothes, eat, rest. And check on Gabrielle. Gabrielle would need him.

Marcel asked for the SAR contact information so he could call them if he needed to, then told Tina, Buffy, and Sascha they should all go and he would call them in the morning.

"I'll call you if I hear anything during the night. Otherwise, see you tomorrow," he said as he opened the car door. His friends got into their cars and waved to him as they pulled out of the parking lot. Marcel waited to give them a good head start before starting his own engine. He was having a hard time mustering up the strength to leave. He felt like he was abandoning his wife, and even though his head said he wasn't, his heart begged to differ.

He drove slowly out of the lot, turning left to get to the Plateau Boulevard then right towards home. After he turned left on Robson, he pulled over to the side of the road and stopped the engine. He gripped the steering wheel with both hands and leaned his head back against the headrest. He needed to gather his thoughts before he got home to Gabrielle. Suddenly his breath caught, and he heaved silently into the cool air, all of his pent-up frustrations and emotions flooding out now he was alone. He bowed his head and covered his face with his hands as the sobs came, wave after wave, his shoulders shuddering with grief. Those shoulders needed to be strong for his daughter. It was best to let out his worry in private.

When the tears stopped a few minutes later, he restarted the car and drove the rest of the way home with renewed purpose - Annette would be found in the morning but Gabrielle needed him now.

Day 2:

Tuesday, November 21ˢᵗ

The motion detector light came on as Marcel pulled the car into the driveway. He pressed the button on the garage door opener, deciding to park in the garage instead of leaving his car in the driveway like he had for the past 17 years. Their garage only had room for one vehicle, and he had insisted Annette use it when she started her dog-walking business because it would contain the dogs as she got them into the van. But her van would not be coming home this night. Parking his car in her space made him feel closer to her.

Marcel got out of the car and shrugged off his light coat. He would take a warmer jacket in the morning. The thought ran through his mind so fast it barely registered, and he immediately felt guilty, knowing Annette didn't have that option, knowing she couldn't opt for a warmer coat or to park her car where she wanted.

He walked up the two steps to the back door of the house and paused. His hands started to shake as he anticipated the flood of feelings he was going to get when he opened the door. Not seeing Chloe rushing to meet him, not having Annette there with a warm hug, knowing his home would feel hollow and empty when he walked in. He fumbled with his keys and tried to gain control so he could get the key into the lock.

As soon as he walked in and saw Gabrielle, he broke down. He was too tired and drained to hide his pain from her. Gabrielle rushed over and held her father. She squeezed him tightly and said, "They're going to find her Dad. It's going to be okay."

"I know Sweetie. We have to be strong," Marcel whispered through sobs as he held her. They had to believe that was true. There were search teams and tomorrow there would be helicopters. They had to have faith!

Nadine and Breanne watched from afar, letting the two embrace in a private family moment. When they finished their hug, Nadine walked toward them, wanting to hold them both but knowing now they only needed each other. There would be time for solace later. "Let's go sit down. You look exhausted, Marcel," she observed aloud.

They all walked into the seating room and Marcel sat near the fireplace to warm up. Gabrielle, Nadine, and Breanne sat on the three-seater couch and looked at Marcel expectantly. They wanted to give him time in case he wanted to share his feelings, but Marcel was introspective.

To break the silence, Gabrielle told him about the visit from the RCMP officer.

"It was awful, Dad! He was walking around the house, looking around the bedroom, and then he came down and sat at the kitchen table. He was being really nice. Talking to me. But you know me, Dad, I don't talk much. We basically just sat there staring at each other. Thank god Nadine showed up!"

Nadine piped in, "Yeah, when I got here they were just sitting there across the table from each other. I think the officer was glad I got here too!" She chuckled, then continued, "after he left, I went upstairs to look around and saw a pile of jewelry on the floor beside Annette's dresser. What's that all about? I can only imagine what he was thinking when he saw that!"

Marcel nodded and explained, "Yesterday Annette was sorting through her jewellery, getting rid of some of the stuff she doesn't wear anymore. She just left it on the floor, not sure what to do with it yet." Marcel looked at the floor and smiled, remembering as Annette chattered while she worked. She told a story about every piece she remembered and commented on every piece she didn't. He'd had to make an excuse to leave the room so he wouldn't have to listen anymore.

He added with a grin, "I wonder if he thought she was looking for the good stuff before skipping the country?" They all chortled amiably, and almost immediately fell back into melancholy. The rain outside reflected their moods perfectly.

Nadine went over her phone call with Annette so Marcel could hear it in person. "I told the officer again how my call with Annette went, that it was pretty much a typical phone call. We had talked for about 20 minutes when Roxy started barking in the background. Annette told me she had to go see why Roxy was barking and hung up. That was the last I heard from her. I have no idea why she was barking, but I know she does that when she sees people on the trails. I just hope it was a person," Nadine told them.

"Yeah, I sure hope so. That's a bit of a mystery. I would love to know what happened after that," Marcel replied.

Nadine went on, "And I always ask Annette about what dogs she has, where she's hiking, that kind of thing. But we got talking about the party last night and I didn't get a chance to ask!" Nadine sounded like she was feeling guilty, though Marcel assured her she had no reason to have regrets.

"The officer must have thought the girls were a little odd. They polished off that ice cream cake that was sitting in the freezer. I think it was good for Gabrielle to get her mind off the search for a bit," Nadine said with a smile and the girls giggled sheepishly. Marcel was pleased to hear about some normal activity rather than the pinpoint focus he'd had on his own worries for the past six hours.

"Sascha stopped in to get the spare van keys. Gabrielle wanted to send some food back for you, so she was searching all over, not sure what to send. She settled on the oranges, figured you needed something healthy. The officer left right after Sascha left," Nadine reported. She was very detail oriented and Marcel was glad she could relate everything he'd missed at home. His own daughter was not nearly so communicative, and right now he needed someone to take the reins of the conversation.

"Yeah, the oranges are still there on the table. I didn't feel much like eating," Marcel said, trying to remember if he'd left them in the anteroom or at the central counter. "It was horrible just sitting in that truck, waiting for something to happen. The searchers sure know what they are doing, very organized, but it is so hard just sitting there."

He shook his head and continued, "They needed the room we were sitting in so the searchers could have a place to warm up. They were starting to come back for a rest and for new assignments. They said they are going to continue searching for a bit longer, but then they would have to call it a night. I've got the number for them, so I can call in for updates."

Marcel sat quietly for a few minutes, starting to get emotional again. Then he took a deep breath, held it in, and exhaled, regaining his composure.

"They'll find her, Dad," Gabrielle said in her soft voice.

"I know sweetie, they'll find her," Marcel said, looking back at her. He was reassuring himself as much as he was reassuring her. The group fell into silence, deep in their own thoughts.

Around 2:00am, Nadine rose and said, "I think it's time we got going. You could probably use some family time." She looked directly at Marcel and added, "Hopefully you can get some sleep. I assume you will be up there at 6:00?"

"Oh yeah, I'll be there. I doubt I will get any sleep though." Marcel replied.

Nadine turned to Gabrielle and said, "You get some sleep honey. Let me know when you wake up and I will come right back here for you."

Gabrielle walked Breanne to the door while Marcel stayed seated and stared into space. Nadine leaned down and whispered quietly to Marcel so the girls wouldn't hear, "The officer also took one of Annette's hair brushes just in case they need a DNA sample. I didn't want the girls to hear that."

Marcel looked at Nadine and said, "That's ok. It won't come to that." But a shudder went though his body. It won't, he told himself again. It can't.

Marcel rose and hugged Nadine, not bothering to thank her because he knew there weren't enough words to express his gratitude for her ever-present friendship. Nadine walked to the door, hugged Gabrielle and said encouragingly, "Hang in there, Honey. They'll find her in the morning."

Gabrielle closed the garage door behind them and returned to her Dad by the fire. He hugged her long and hard. "They will find her…" he said softly, again. She sat on the couch, Marcel took the chair by the fire, and the two sat in sombre silence.

Seeing Gabrielle's eyes starting to droop, Marcel said gently, "Lay down, sweetheart. I'll wake you if I hear anything." He took a blanket from the armrest and laid it over Gabrielle as she got comfortable on the couch. Soon she was breathing smoothly and softly. Marcel sat in the chair by the fire and watched his beautiful daughter slumber. She looked so peaceful, so restful. He wished he could slip away mentally, even momentarily, but his mind raced with questions. He wondered what it would be like for Annette right now, how cold she was, if the dogs were keeping her warm. He wondered if she'd found shelter, if she was hurt, if she was afraid. HE was afraid.

At 2:40am, Marcel got up and went to his office upstairs. He sat at his desk and opened his computer, which needed to be rebooted because of the power outage. Once it was up and running, he typed out an email to his boss who is also a good friend:

"I wanted to let you know that Annette has been missing on eagle mountain since last night. RCMP, then search and rescue have been searching since 7, but no sign of her yet. I will not be in the office Tuesday and will likely take the rest of the week off. I will let you know when there is an update."

He hit SEND and closed his computer, knowing his company would understand and give him the time he needed. He'd worked there for 26 years because they were good to him and always treated their employees fairly. He was confident they would support him in every way so he could focus on his family in this crazy situation. It WAS crazy, there was no other way to describe it. It wasn't tragic yet – no tragedy had been discovered – but it was a mystery, and yes, unimaginable and crazy!

Marcel walked aimlessly into their bedroom. He saw the pile of jewellery on the floor where Annette had placed them while she sorted through them. He walked over and sat on the carpet with his back leaning against their bed. He picked up a ring from the pile and studied it. It wasn't familiar, but then, he wasn't the type of guy to notice things like that. He put the ring down and twirled his wedding ring around his own finger. That was the only piece of jewellery which had ever meant anything to him, and it was the closest thing he had to touching Annette.

He sat there for a long time thinking about Annette. He could picture her walking around the bedroom, hear her telling him to "turn off that computer and get to bed!" His heart ached for her. He couldn't stay there, it felt too empty. He returned to his chair by the fireplace and sat, watching his beautiful daughter sleep.

At 3:30, Marcel had to call the SAR truck. He couldn't wait any longer, he just needed something. Anything.

"Mike, it's Marcel. How's it going? Have you found anything?" He was unable to hide the desperation seeping into his voice.

Mike was surprised to hear from him but answered honestly, "No, nothing yet. The teams are all on their way back in, wrapping up for the night. I'm sorry, Marcel, we didn't see any sign of her or the dogs." He sounded truly disappointed. There was no question in Marcel's mind, these people really want to find her. This is what they do, what they live for.

"Ok Mike, I understand." Marcel said dejectedly.

"We will be back up here in the morning at 6:00. It's a school day so the command truck can't park at the school. We will be in the Westwood Plateau Golf Club parking lot. There will be fresh search crews too. The Coquitlam team is exhausted so will be taking the day off. We should be able to get the helicopters up too. Don't worry, Marcel, we'll find her," he said with confidence.

"Thanks, Mike, I know you will. Thank you for everything you've done. Good night," Marcel said quietly, and hung up the phone. He covered his mouth with his hand as if that would hold back his emotions, but the tears stung his eyes anyway.

He walked over to the couch where Gabrielle was sleeping and sat on the coffee table watching her sleep. Things were always less painful when you slept, he mused. After a few moments he stroked her head and woke her up as gently as he could.

"What time is it," she asked. "Did they find her?"

"No, sweetie, not yet. They are finished for the night though. They will be starting again at 6:00. It will be so much easier in the daylight. They will find her tomorrow." Marcel said, with more bravado than he felt.

"I want you to go up to bed. You need to get your sleep," he encouraged.

"What about you, Dad? You need your sleep too," Gabrielle pleaded.

"I'm going to stay here on the couch. I'll be ok. I just can't go to bed right now. I want you to get some sleep and call me as soon as you wake up. I don't want you being alone right now," he said.

"I will, Dad. Good night," she hugged and kissed him before trotting up the stairs to her bedroom.

"Good night, sweetie. I love you," Marcel yelled after her.

"I love you too, Dad," she called down the stairs.

Marcel got the alarm clock from their bedroom. If he slept, he sure didn't want to sleep in. He set the alarm for 5:45am, an hour and a half away. He put the clock on the coffee table, laid down and put the blanket over himself.

Sleep would not come, however. He stared into the fire. Time slipped by silently while he lay thinking about what Annette was doing now. What the dogs were doing. Hoping they were just lost, that they would walk out in the morning. What happened? The house, the car, his job. None of it meant anything without Annette.

The world was still dark at 5:30 when Marcel got up to shower. The past few hours had been restless and sleepless, so showering was a better use of his time than staring into the fire. He needed to shake the cobwebs before going to the mountain. After his shower he looked out the bedroom window and saw the weather had only worsened through the night. He dressed in warm clothes, grabbed a thick jacket, and headed out to his car.

It would take less than 5 minutes to get to the golf course, which was only a few blocks up the hill past where they had been last night, at the school. He arrived at 5:45 to find the only gate into the golf club closed and a media truck waiting. He did a u-turn and parked his car across the street and waited.

Ten minutes later, the SAR command truck pulled up to the gate. The truck idled in place for a few minutes, then drove away, the CBC media van in hot pursuit. Marcel did another u-turn and followed the trucks up the hill toward the lot where Annette's van was parked. Their little procession rolled slowly up the access road and the SAR pulled into the only flat spot large enough to hold it. Marcel parked his car across the road from the van, not wanting to be in their way. The search crews would be arriving soon and they'd need room. Within minutes, four more news vans had arrived and were getting set up.

Marcel got out of his car and looked up at the sky. The rain was slushy and relentless, the air bitter cold. He looked to the horizon and there was no end to the ominous clouds. It was a grey and blustery day, and he wondered how anyone could survive an entire night outside in such conditions. It seemed impossible, but he knew Annette was one tough lady. She'd survived tough situations before, he had to believe she would survive this too. The mental strength and fortitude it took to deal with multiple miscarriages was only one example of how resilient she was!

He looked up the paved service road for the grounds keepers and walked slowly along it. This was a great trail for dogs and dog walkers because it was unencumbered and wide, perfect for dogs with short legs. After he'd walked some ways, maybe 100 feet, he stopped. He whistled for Chloe, knowing she would come running if she could hear him. Only silence greeted him.

Marcel didn't bother calling for Annette, he knew she wouldn't hear him. Instead he whispered to her, "We're coming, baby. Hold on. Help us find you."

Then the tears came again. This time he was on his own so there was no need to hold anything back. He had to let it out freely, without an audience. When he felt the pressure was released, he sucked it up, wiped his eyes, and walked back to the truck to watch people come in. Wanting to stay out of the way but not wanting to get out of the rain, he sat on the back bumper of the SAR command truck and watched everyone arrive. News crews, volunteers, and RCMP members appeared.

As he watched the action, the Facebook app sent a notification to his phone, so Marcel checked his messages. There was a message from their old friend Theresa! There was a time when they spent holidays and vacations together, but it seemed they'd drifted apart over the past few years. Well-meaning "let's get together" promises which never materialized had allowed them to lose touch, but they'd never stopped caring for each other. Marcel was so happy to hear from her now. Theresa asked where he was, so he typed his location. She replied immediately and told him she was coming straight away. He knew there was nothing he could say to stop her – when she had her mind set on something there was no stopping her, and he was glad. He needed the company of strong people right now who would hold him up when his faith started to falter.

Marcel sat on the bumper and watched as the news crews set up under an e-z up canopy. The search crews started to arrive now, and the little parking lot was filling up quickly. Soon people would have to start parking down on Plateau Boulevard and walking up.

Ian MacDonald, the guy in charge of the search today, opened the truck door and waved Marcel into the command centre. He went in and met some new search managers – the previous night's crew were resting up at home before going back out to search. They showed him on the maps where they would be concentrating their search that morning, then asked him to provide Annette's information again. Marcel reiterated the details – what she was wearing, what she had with her, what type of person she was, what kinds of dogs she had with her. They probably had all that information already but sometimes more details come out when a story is repeated, so it made sense for them to ask him to repeat it. He didn't mind at all, he loved talking about Annette.

Ian was hopeful the helicopters would be able to join the search later that day, but it was weather-dependent.

"There are two helicopters that could search today," he told Marcel. "The first is RCMP Air-1. This is the RCMP helicopter that has FLIR or Forward Looking Infra Red. It allows the operator to see heat signatures in the forest. The second is the yellow helicopter belonging to a private company SAR calls in when we need a chopper. The owner, Peter

Murray, is a good friend of mine. They are very reliable. Unfortunately, it doesn't have FLIR, but they are pretty experienced in searching. If the weather lifts a bit, we should see them in the air once it gets light out."

"Thanks for the update, Ian. Let's cross our fingers the helicopters can fly today. Thanks for everything," Marcel said, feeling like he was on repeat. He couldn't stop thanking the searchers, but also knew he could never say enough thank-yous.

Marcel's cellphone rang so he stepped outside to answer it. His sister Janette was calling to let him know the family was praying for them. Was there anything they could do for him? Marcel asked her to go be with their father who was 88 and still lived on his own. He and Annette had an especially close relationship and Marcel knew this news would hit him hard. Janette promised she would go and stay with him until this ordeal was over.

After they hung up, he stood outside the command truck and watched as the search crews made preparations and the media gave whatever updates they could to their stations. He knew he'd have to give them a statement, so he composed himself and walked over to their tent. They gathered around him, breathlessly waiting for comment.

He tried to put on a brave face and sound positive, saying things like, "She's done these trails many times, she knows these trails," and "She typically comes up here when she has the older dogs because it's easier trails." It was becoming increasingly difficult for Marcel to get the words out. He took deep breaths to calm his nerves and steady his emotions but try as he might his voice still wavered when he spoke. He pleaded to other hikers, "If you find anybody on the mountain, grab them and bring them down."

The media people were kind and supportive, offering words of encouragement and asking questions which weren't too personal. They asked about his thoughts on the search and Marcel told them, "I have to give them a chance to do what they do, they are professionals, I'm not." He added "I need to be where they are so I can hear if anything… anything happens… ummm… they have crews coming out from all over the lower mainland."

RCMP Corporal Michael McLaughlin joined the interview and told the news crews, "We're obviously very concerned. The bush is heavy, the weather is bad with the rain and the cold. This is something we need to address right away." He went on to say the police didn't have any reason to believe there was "foul play or anything nefarious going on."

Coquitlam Search and Rescue manager Ian MacDonald told the reporters, "One of the dogs is 13 years old and we've been told that it can only go for about two hours. That also leads us to suspect that that's the dog causing trouble and it's probably just decided not to move anymore."

A reporter asked Ian why they haven't seen any sign of the dogs. He replied, "That perplexes us, it perplexes the RCMP, I think it perplexes the dog walking community." It was also of grave concern for Marcel, who knew the dogs were capable and strong, and their absence was alarming.

Marcel perched on the back bumper of the SAR truck and listened while the news crews gave their reports in their cameras. He heard them refer to Annette as a 52-year-old lost in the woods, which made him smile because he knew 56-year-old Annette would get a kick out of that.

He sat there in the slushy rain for a long time because it didn't feel right to get out of the rain. He wanted to feel what Annette was feeling, as if in some small way that would bring him closer to her.

Tuesday, November 21st, 6:15am

The morning light crept in slowly. From dark silhouettes, the dogs' shapes emerged. With each blink, Annette could see the dogs clearer. It was still dark, but she could see Chloe's eyes watching her, glinting in the scant light of dawn.

Icy rain fell onto her face and she could feel her hair stiffening in the cold. She could see her breath, which was a small comfort – it meant her core was warmer than the air. The rain felt like pin pricks on her face and she turned her head to the side as if doing so would stop it from hurting.

Both dogs rose to their feet as they saw Annette stirring. She gathered all her strength and rolled to her right side. That small movement knocked the wind out of her and she paused, catching her breath and bracing for exertion. She yelled out in pain as she pulled her left knee up preparing to roll forward onto her stomach. If she could just get up onto all fours, she could manage to stand. She held her breath and swung her body forward onto her elbows and knees.

She hung her head down between her arms and stretched her neck. Her body ached from the fall but also from laying still on the hard ground for over 12 hours. Moving her right knee hurt less so she pulled it up under her chest and gave a karate yell as she pushed herself to standing. Once upright, she could feel the wind rushing at her, blowing the rain sideways. She was stiff and soaked, but she was still alive and somewhat mobile. And motivated. She would find Bubba if it killed her.

Chloe and Roxy wagged their tails and looked at her happily. Annette didn't want to disappoint them if they thought they were going home today, so best to get moving and find Bubba. There were two things they needed to accomplish that morning: find Bubba and find their way out. The light was coming up fast now and she could see past more than just a few trees. Which way should they go? She had no idea. But she was in no condition to be climbing hills or logs, so she chose the easiest way, the one with no impediments.

"Bubba! Where are you, buddy?" she called as loudly as she could while she hobbled between logs and trees. The dogs anticipated her movements and leapt ahead, seemingly in a hurry to get out of there too. It was much easier to see now that it was light out, and Annette knew the other dogs would find Bubba if he was anyplace near.

It didn't take long before Bubba appeared. He must have been close by and seemed none the worse for wear. His scars must've been more emotional, as he didn't leave Annette's side for the rest of the day.

Spending the night alone surely gave him a fright and now he was glued to her. "Well, that's good," thought Annette.

With one task completed, her next task was to find their way back to the van. Annette knew if she could find the power lines, they could easily get to the van. But which way is it to the powerlines? There were no openings visible and no points of reference. And she was in so much pain it was hard to think straight! Was she supposed to stay put? Go uphill? Go downhill? Follow the sun? All she knew is she couldn't sit still and do nothing, so she kept them moving forward.

Where ever the terrain was easiest, that's where they walked. Annette looked for signs of a clearing, perhaps marking the powerline or a larger trail, but most clearings were simply trees knocked over by the wind or diseased roots. She stopped when she heard booms. She cocked an ear to listen for the shots from the gun club, but the booms echoed and she couldn't tell where they were coming from. They were distant, and when she thought they were to the left, she heard them again on the right. It was a red herring, just like the clearings. She pressed forward.

Tuesday, November 21st, 6:30am

Marcel watched as SAR volunteers arrived, picked up their assignments, and headed out. He quietly thanked them and asked god to watch out for them. The rain was not letting up and it was going to be a rough one out there today.

A friendly face walked up the road. Theresa grabbed Marcel in a bear hug and asked if there was anything she could do for him. "Just being here is a big help," Marcel replied as he held her tightly. It was so good to see his old friend again.

"Tell me everything when you're ready," she said, knowing he would confide in her when he was mentally and emotionally able.

They stood under the awning of the command centre truck and watched as a tow truck came and hooked up Annette's van. Marcel supposed it was now a crime scene and would be towed to the police compound for evidence. He knew there were a few bags of old clothes in the back of the van which was on its way to the thrift shop, but Annette hadn't gotten around to donating them yet. What might the police make of that, he wondered?

Another old friend came out of the woodwork. His good friend Stuart called at 7:17am. They hadn't seen each other in quite a while but Stuart had heard about Annette's disappearance on the news and wanted to help. He was an outdoor enthusiast so had all his gear packed up and was ready to start searching. He was heading up there now. Marcel doubted he would be allowed onto the mountain but didn't try to discourage him. It would be great to have his friendly face around him. Stuart was someone who wouldn't let people get in his way, and Marcel respected that.

Nadine showed up about then, despite having left Marcel's house only 5 hours ago. She hugged him tearfully and asks if there was any news. Marcel looked down and shook his head no.

Now, Bubba's owner, Tina, walked up the road. She greeted everyone with a sad smile and gave Marcel a hug. "Any news?" Again, Marcel shook his head.

Sascha had come to show his support for Marcel but he couldn't stay this time. He needed to go to work, even though he knew he wouldn't be able to concentrate on anything work related. After he and Buffy had left the school's parking lot last night, they had gone home only to watch Eagle

Mountain from their windows. They could see the headlamps of the searchers scattered on the mountainside, a disturbing yet comforting sight. They couldn't sleep knowing Annette was out there somewhere in the dark and cold forest.

"It's okay, I'll call you if there's anything," Marcel said, thanking his friend for stopping by. Marcel was feeling very grateful for all his friends' support, it felt good to have people around him who knew and cared about Annette too.

Stuart arrived looking like a Mountain Equipment Coop advertisement, decked out in all the gear anyone could ever need in the bush. He looked more like a SAR volunteer than the SAR volunteers! Marcel was impressed with Stuart's preparedness and was grateful to have a true friend joining the search. No one else would be reporting to Marcel directly, but Stuart would bring him all the info he could gather.

With emotional reunions and a lack of sleep clouding his brain, Marcel needed to steal away for a few minutes to gather his thoughts. He slipped away from his friends and headed back up the path where he'd walked earlier. He walked along slowly, thinking and praying. When he turned to go back, he found Nadine following him at a respectful distance.

"I'm sorry, I didn't want to disturb you, but I didn't want to leave you alone either," she smiled apologetically. They walked toward each other and entered into a tearful embrace and held it for a long time.

"She sure likes to keep things exciting, doesn't she," Marcel said as they broke the hug. They often joked about how Annette was always the life of the party, stirring things up, making it fun. They both chuckled.

As they headed back to the command truck, Marcel wished everyone had friends like these.

It was 9:28 when Marcel got a text message from his brother Gerald in Victoria. He would be on the 11:30am ferry to Vancouver and would call him when he got closer, around 2:00. Gerald is a retired RCMP officer and Marcel was looking forward to getting his guidance and support.

Shortly after, Gabrielle called Marcel. He stepped away from his friends to take the call. There wasn't much to tell her, but he said the search teams had already been searching for a few hours. He could tell from her quiet tone she had expected it to all be over by now and was disappointed with the news.

Marcel walked back to his friends, took Nadine aside, and asked, "Can you go back to the house and stay with Gabrielle? I don't want her to be alone right now." Nadine nodded, happy to have a job rather than standing around in the freezing rain feeling helpless.

Next to arrive was Buffy, but she called and said the RCMP at the gate wouldn't allow her in because the lot was getting crowded and the SAR needed room for their people to park. Marcel told Buffy to hand her phone to the officer. Marcel said, "Hi, this is Marcel, Annette Poitras' husband. Buffy is a close friend of ours and I really need the support right now. Could you please allow her in?"

"No problem, sir. I will just ask her to park down the street and she can walk up," he replied. Marcel thanked him and could hear Buffy thanking him as well. One more person to lean on.

With the search crews gone, there was room for Marcel and his friends in the SAR truck's anteroom. The radio sat on the table, but it remained quiet. Marcel sat with Theresa, Tina, and Buffy in comfortable silence. Their presence was all that Marcel needed right now; inane chatter would have agitated him. They watched the rain pelting the windows, thankful there was no more snow mixed in with the precipitation. They watched as an RCMP officer walked down the powerline trail holding a shotgun on his hip, pointing up, and hoped they were just being cautious and no one had seen a bear.

The thought of bears raised the same questions again: Why haven't we heard the dogs? What happened after Annette disconnected her call with Nadine? What was Roxy barking at? Was there a bear? A cougar? Even worse, did someone harm her? Unanswered questions swirled in their heads and came out of their mouths because there was nothing else to say.

An RCMP corporal stuck his head in the truck and asked to speak to Marcel outside. Marcel leapt up. Was there news? Had they found her?

The corporal was sorry he'd raised Marcel's hopes and had nothing to tell him, he merely needed to get more information. He explained they were doing everything they could, and part of that search routine was to handle it like every other missing persons investigation.

"We would look pretty foolish if five days from now we learned that Annette wasn't on the mountain and we hadn't started a proper investigation yet," Corporal Mike McLaughlin said.

"I understand," Marcel nodded. "I have nothing to hide."

"First I need your banking information. Can you tell me what bank you deal with? Which is your branch?" he asked. Marcel gave him the information he needed.

Then the Corporal asked, "Do you have any vacation plans? Any charges for anything related to travel?" They were obviously looking to see if Annette might have skipped the country. Had they already checked the accounts, seen the charges, and were testing Marcel to see if he would mention them? Marcel told him about their planned family vacation to London to visit Annette's father during Christmas. They would see the payment in their accounts.

Marcel completely understood and was very forthcoming. He knew the sooner they ruled out other possibilities they would concentrate their efforts on where he knew she was – in the forest where they were standing! He had nothing, NOTHING, to hide.

Then the officer asked something which made Marcel balk.

"Do you think there is a possibility Annette met someone on the mountain and they left in that person's car? Maybe they went for a hike someplace else?" Mike asked.

"Not likely. That would be out of character for her, especially since she has dogs. If she went anywhere else she would have taken the van," Marcel told the officer with absolute certainty.

Mike thanked Marcel for his time and Marcel thanked him for everything the RCMP were doing. He was grateful to have professionals taking control and doing what needed to be done.

As Marcel was about to go back into the truck, he heard a whup whup whup. He looked up to see two helicopters flying in from the south – a yellow Talon and the RCMP Air 1. Marcel's spirits lifted as he watched them scouring the forest for any signs of Annette or the dogs.

The weather had lifted just enough for the helicopters to be able to fly, but even though Marcel had been told drones could be an option, the weather was still too harsh to use them. He was told this was the exact location where the SAR had been training with their drones, and he remembered seeing them in the past when he'd walked up here. The weather really was not cooperating…

Marcel returned to the truck and sat with his friends, telling them what had transpired. They had all been bracing themselves for news – good or bad – but were happy to hear progress was being made.

At 10:08 Marcel sent his office an email update. He wrote:

"Just a quick update with no real news. Lots of search crews out and more arriving all the time. Helicopter is up, and they are going to bring in drones to search. At this point I just have to wait and trust in the professionals."

The foursome sat and waited. They felt useless, but there was nothing they could do that wasn't already being done. Through small talk and occasional tears, they held out hope. Whatever the outcome was going to be, they needed to stay strong. For Marcel, for Gabrielle, for all of them.

Marcel looked out the window and saw his neighbours Elisa and David walking up the road toward the truck. He got up and went outside to greet them.

"How did you get past the gate?" he asked them as they hugged each other.

"We just told them we were family," David laughed. They were determined to get up to Marcel and show him support. "Hang in there, they're going to find her," David said as he patted Marcel's shoulder. Marcel nodded, sighed, and gave a weak smile to his friends.

There wasn't room in the truck for everyone, so Marcel and his neighbours stood under the truck's awning chatting. They watched what was going on, asked a few questions about the search, but didn't stay too long. They didn't want Marcel to feel obligated to stand with them and socialize when he was in so much turmoil. They told him they'd keep an eye on things at home and would be at the ready if Marcel needed anything. Elisa and Dave left with more hugs and comments like "They will find her."

Shortly after they left, a uniformed city by-law officer appeared at Marcel's side with a bag of submarine sandwiches from Subway and a tray of drinks.

"JOHN," Marcel blurted loudly, surprised to see his friend. John was a good friend from way back. Before John worked for the city, Annette and John used to volunteer at a nearby SPCA. They would go every morning and walk as many dogs as they could in the over-crowded shelter, quite often bending the rules of one dog per walker, just to make sure all the dogs got some time out of their cages. They both did everything they could to help those dogs, and formed a friendship based on their mutual love and respect for dogs.

John followed Marcel with the food and drinks into the trailer where they made room for him to sit on the bench. Marcel sat at the table and took one of the iced teas for himself. He couldn't eat but the iced tea was perfect. He sipped it, grateful for the cool liquid but also happy to have something to hold, something to focus on.

It was slow going for all of them. The dogs no longer jumped over logs, they went around them like Annette. She could tell they were tired and hungry, and she desperately wanted to save them from this hell.

Annette stopped. "Bubba, where are you?" she hollered. She turned around to find him at her heels. "Good boy," she said, smiling meekly at him. Having him staying close to her was one less thing she had to worry about.

As they walked slowly, and Annette boosted Bubba over logs, things started to feel familiar. Had they already crossed this log? Didn't they pass that large stump a while ago? Were they walking around in circles? They had gone neither up nor down in elevation as far as she could tell, but if anything, they would walk downhill. It was unlikely to circle back if you kept going downhill… wasn't it?

She didn't know anymore. All she could think about was the dogs who'd be showing up to her house this morning and she wasn't there to take them in. And what about Ben, who was coming early for her to take him to school? What must Marcel be thinking??

What was that thumping noise? Distant but becoming louder. Helicopter! Marcel must have sent it to look for her! She waved at it as it hovered nearby, but they probably couldn't see her if they weren't directly above her. The yellow helicopter flew over her periodically, but she didn't know if they had spotted her. She kept moving.

A different helicopter buzzed overhead, this time an RCMP one. She waved and yelled, but it too flew past. With each encounter, she grew more frustrated and angry. "Why can't you see me?" she yelled at the choppers. "I'm right HERE!" she screamed as she took off her pink raincoat and waved it at them. The canopy was too thick, the sky was too grey, and she was too small.

Four hours after he left, Marcel saw Stuart walking down the access road toward them. He didn't look like a man who had found a missing person, but he looked excited about something. Marcel got up and met him outside the truck. They stood under the awning out of the rain and Stuart pulled his cell phone out of his waterproof pocket.

"Hey, buddy. Sorry, no sign of her yet," he said with disappointment. "I headed up the ridge toward Cypress Lake. I hooked up with one of the search teams up there. I don't think they were too excited to have me along, but once they realized I was properly equipped and seemed to know what I was doing, they let me tag along. A good group of people! We didn't get as far as the lake before we had to turn back, but let me show you what I found…"

He showed Marcel pictures he had taken of the little camps he had come across on the mountain. People had built make-shift shacks and abandoned them – not fancy but offering shelter from the rain if nothing else. Marcel hoped Annette had found one and was staying dry while she waited to be rescued.

"I'm going to take a rest for a while, then head out again. Hopefully I can get in with another team this afternoon," he said.

Marcel thanked him again for making the effort. Stuart was a man of action who would not sit and let other people do the work. He also had a soft spot for Annette and was going to do everything he could for her. He had a heart of gold.

Marcel noticed people arriving with big boxes of bagged lunches for the searchers, more volunteers the public never hears about. He went into the truck's anteroom and asked his friends to join him outside. He assumed the search teams would be coming back to eat and rest, and he wanted them to be comfortable. After all, they were volunteering their time here when they should be working at their regular jobs, earning money for their own families. Instead they were here, dedicating their time to try putting HIS family back together. He was beyond grateful and humbled, and giving them room to warm up and rest was the least he could do!

Exhaustion was catching up to him. Now was a good time to go home and be with Gabrielle. He needed to see her, to hold her.

"Hey guys, I need to go home for a bit. I think you guys need the rest too. I sure appreciate you spending your day with me, I really needed the help," he said, his voice cracking with emotion. Theresa offered to drive

Marcel home, predicting he would be too tired and emotional to drive safely. Marcel gratefully accepted the offer.

Theresa dug her car keys out of her pocket and the two headed down the hill to her car. Theresa could see how spent Marcel was, so she opened the passenger's door and guided him in with a hand on his elbow. The drive home was quiet, both of them knowing words would not bring Annette back.

When she heard the door open, Gabrielle rushed to her Dad. She knew there was no news and she could see in his face how desperate he was becoming. He grabbed onto her and held her, his shoulders shaking as the tears streamed down his face. She rubbed his back and let him lean on her – she was taller than her mother and could hold her father up if she needed to.

But she didn't need to. Instead, she led him upstairs to rest. Marcel laid down on the bed, instinctively taking his usual side. Gabrielle lay down next to him, on her side, facing him. She begged him to sleep, talked to him in a low, soothing voice. Marcel drifted off momentarily, but he was unable to fully relax. He held Gabrielle's hand and that was all the medicine he needed. Laying with her there was enough to recharge him and keep him going for a while longer.

At 2:00pm, Marcel realized his brother would be there soon, but wouldn't know where to find him. He sent him a quick text saying, *"Gerald, I am at home when you get into town."*

Within ten seconds the door bell rang, and Marcel was out of bed like a shot. He raced down the stairs hoping to receive good news from the RCMP. It was the RCMP all right, but it was his brother Gerald arriving from Victoria. Of course he was able to find Marcel – the RCMP always get their man!

Disappointment and relief and grief all culminated as Marcel tumbled into his brother's arms. Gerald hugged him hard and both men cried. Gerald had supported Marcel through every tough time in the past, and he would be there for his little brother every time in the future.

Gerald left his suitcase on the living room floor. They would work out sleeping arrangements later, if indeed there would be any sleeping to be done. He doubted it. Gerald suggested they head back up to the base camp so he could get an idea of what was going on – he'd had vast experience in this type of thing so he knew what Marcel needed. Aside from having his family around him, he also needed to be at the site in case something happened.

Gabrielle and Nadine stayed behind while Theresa drove Gerald and

Marcel back up to the mountain and the three parked on Plateau Boulevard so the car wouldn't be in anyone's way. As they walked up the road toward the base camp, Marcel's eyes searched for someone who could give them an update. No one was in sight, so they entered the SAR truck and found Ian there. Marcel introduced Gerald and the two men shook hands as Ian told them what was new.

While Marcel had been home, a man named Marc had come forward about a sighting of Annette. "The RCMP got the call about an hour ago," Ian told them. "The gentleman told us that he bumped into Annette on the trail Monday afternoon." Marcel and Gerald listened intently.

"He said he was walking down the trail when a boxer came running up to him barking. Shortly after, a lady came along and call the dog off. She told him the dog would just bark but wouldn't bite."

Marcel interrupted, "Please, tell me again. Exactly what did she say to him?"

"I understand she said, *'I'm really sorry, she just barks, she won't bite'*," he clarified. Marcel held up his hand in a silent request to stop there. It took a few moments to collect himself before he could speak again, the emotions making the words catch in his throat. It was almost like he could hear her saying those words. He had known her for 25 years and knew exactly how she spoke. He knew for a fact those are the words she would have used. There was no doubt in his mind that this man had seen Annette.

"That was her," Marcel said, "I know that was her he saw."

Ian continued, "He says he saw her at around 2:30 in this area," and he pointed to a place on the map about a half hour walk northwest from where they stood. "He didn't talk to her, just continued on his walk. This is a good thing, we can now place Annette at a specific place at a specific time. This has helped us to focus our search."

Finally, the mystery of Roxy's barking had been solved! They had wracked their brains trying to figure out what Roxy had been barking at when Annette was on the phone with Nadine. Now they knew. There was nothing untoward, no danger. Roxy was simply barking at a stranger.

Not only that, but now they had confirmation Annette had definitely been on the mountain and hadn't gotten into another vehicle and driven away. It was what Marcel had known all along, but now the SAR team had good reason to continue their search.

In a case like this where every little bit of information is helpful, this information was crucial. They now had a focus for their search. They knew she hadn't gone east, which is where they had searched first, and that ground was well covered. South of the sighting locale the terrain was steep and rough – it was unlikely she would go that way especially with Bubba. North and west would now be their focus, as those were the directions with the easiest walking trails.

Marcel said a silent thank you to Marc. This was the first time since yesterday evening Marcel had good reason to hope for the best.

He and Gerald thanked Ian for his update and walked back to the anteroom to give Tina and Buffy the good news. They all agreed this was a good sign, and the aura at the table was noticeably lighter for a few minutes. Their excitement soon faded back to worry, as they recognized this didn't diminish the fact it was a scary situation – yes, she had been seen; yes, she was still on the mountain; but she had now been out there for over 24 hours with no food or shelter, as far as they knew. Had they run into a bear? Had she fallen into a river? Was one of the dogs hurt? Marcel knew she would never leave one of the dogs out there alone, and while he hated to think about that stubborn streak of hers, it was also one of the things he admired about her.

It had been nine hours since he'd last spoken to the media. He was grateful for their presence because they were a symbol of hope – as long as they were there waiting for a story, the story stayed alive. Marcel wanted to remind people Annette was tough, he didn't want them to give up looking for her. He walked out to their media tent and tried to sound hopeful. Inside he was drowning in fear. After a brief interview, Marcel stopped to collect himself before facing his family and friends again.

Back inside the truck, Gerald was busy looking down at his phone. He looked up at Marcel and asked, "Do you feel like having company?" Marcel raised his eyebrows in question.

"There's a truckload of family coming down from Kelowna, they'll be here this evening. Andy, Maurice, Janette and Loren are driving down." Gerald told him. Loren was Janette's husband and the other three were Marcel's siblings.

Reinforcements were on their way! Wasn't it just like his family to come running when he needed them. Marcel is the youngest of eight children, with four brothers and three sisters. He referred to himself as the #1 Son – from the bottom up! Or when he was feeling cocky he would say they didn't stop having kids until they reached perfection. He often marvelled at his parents' decision to have such a large family, and now he was sure glad they did.

Their family was very close, and everyone came running when one of them was in trouble. Marcel loved being part of a large family and it was times like these when he appreciated it the most.

"Did you want them to get a hotel room?" asked Gerald, thinking he knew the answer but wanting to double check in case Marcel needed some space.

"Hell no! I need them now. I have lots of room at the house, we will figure it out. I'm glad to have them," Marcel said.

They continued to sit and wait in silence, knowing time was against them as daylight would soon begin to fade.

"Chloe, come!" Annette called to her border collie. She was running too far up ahead and with the fog rolling in, it was getting harder to keep track of the dogs. She needed them to stick close to her, but Chloe kept running further as if she was looking for a way out. Maybe she knew the way?

The rain had gotten heavier, if that was even possible. Annette was soaked to the bone and exhausted, her energy completely spent. She wanted to sit and rest but sensed it would be getting dark soon so wanted to keep moving. There was still a chance she could stumble across the powerline and find her way back to the van before dark. Where was that powerline?!

"And why can't those helicopters see this pink jacket I'm waving?" she yelled into the canopy. The trees ignored her, swaying ominously in the wind as if dancing at her funeral. The sound of the helicopter faded away again.

They walked slowly – very slowly – for another hour or so. Maybe it was two hours. It was hard to tell the time of day in the gloom of the forest. She was growing more uncoordinated with each passing minute, having to hold onto trees just to step over roots. Why did there have to be so many roots and downed trees? And so big! Annette noticed it had been quite a while since she'd last heard a helicopter, and it was starting to get dark. She couldn't believe she had to spend another night outside. This realization brought her to her knees.

Annette simply could not move any longer. She looked nearby for any kind of shelter – a large stump, a downed tree, a foxhole, anything. Finding no place within crawling distance which would offer protection, she resigned herself to laying on the ground right where she was, next to a large log. Annette heard snuffling and turned her head to see Bubba scratching at the ground. She watched as Bubba scraped away the dead leaves and sticks underneath a fern. He had made himself a dry nest! What a great idea!

She was too big to fit under a fern, so Annette brushed away the wet debris as well as she could from as much ground as she could reach between her and the log. The pain in her side made moving her arms unbearable, her arms wet and heavy from rain and exhaustion. When she couldn't expend any more energy, she planted her bum into the shallow pit and dragged her legs over to lay down. She pulled her hood up and cinched it tight so forest debris couldn't fall down her neck, then laid back into her hole.

Unable to lay on her side or pull her knees up, Annette lay flat on the ground with her arms crossed upon her chest. For the first time since noon the previous day, Annette had the urge to pee. The thought of having to get up, undo her pants, and squat was ridiculous. Utterly laughable. She couldn't stand up let alone pull her pants down. Or squat, for that matter. No, she was too weary to be concerned with propriety or sanitation. This situation had caused her more indignity than simply peeing in her pants!

She felt the warmth trickle between her legs. There wasn't much. She couldn't have cared less.

Ian, that day's SAR manager, came to the anteroom to give Marcel and Gerald an update.

"Hey Marcel, let me show you our progress today," he said, inviting the men to join him in the control centre of the truck where all the information was compiled. He pointed to a large chart they had up on the wall, a topographical map of the area centered around where Annette's van was found. It showed the quarry to the east, residential neighbourhoods and golf course to the south, Cypress Mountain to the west, and Eagle Mountain to the far west. The Coquitlam Watershed was outlined to the north. The map was riddled with coloured lines, some running straight and others squiggling across the map.

"Each team member who goes out has a GPS tracker on them," he explained. "When they get back from their assigned task area, we upload the data from their tracker and plot it on the map. Different search areas have different colors."

"You can even see the tracking from the SAR helicopter, which also has a GPS tracker. That's the white line that goes all over the place. Unfortunately, the RCMP helicopter does not have GPS tracking," he added regrettably.

"This morning we focused on Task Area 6," he continued, and pointed to the area around the quarry. "We are even sending a team down Pipeline Road looking in ditches and places she may have hunkered down for the night." Pipeline Road ran alongside the Coquitlam River, in the valley between Eagle Mountain and Burke Mountain. If Annette had followed the powerlines down, she could have reached that road. Though the road was long, there wasn't much traffic at that point as it led to an area with restricted access and the roadsides were forested.

"If you look here," he said pointing to Area 9 on the side of Cypress Mountain, "you can see where the gentleman reported seeing her. That has really helped us to focus our search," he added, sounding hopeful. "If you look at the lines of elevation, you will see they are very close together to the west of there. We feel that terrain is too steep for her to have climbed it." Marcel nodded in agreement, certain Annette would stay in an area where it was easier for Bubba to walk with his short legs.

Ian continued, "To the north it is fairly flat, with a slight slope down all the way to the watershed. You can see all the GPS tracks where the teams have searched, heading north from that point." He pointed to Area 8.

Gerald gave Marcel's shoulder a pat of reassurance. It was encouraging to see how much progress had been made in less than 24 hours. Marcel was pleased and grateful for their time and efforts but was not prepared for what he heard next.

"Unfortunately, it is starting to get dark and the weather is getting a lot worse. We are going to wind down the search for the night." Ian said solemnly but matter-of-factly.

Marcel's heart sank. He looked at Ian and asked, "By 'wind down', do you mean 'stop the search'?"

Ian shook his head emphatically. "No, we're not giving up. Not at all. But we have completed the search through the most accessible areas and now we are going to have to get into some very rugged terrain, where it's far too dangerous to search at night."

He leaned against the counter and faced the men squarely. "The teams are tired and cold and it's time to bring them in. We have to consider the crew's safety. Tomorrow we will bring in fresh teams to resume the search."

Ian turned back to the map. "There are two areas here and here," he said, pointing to the north western tip of Task Area 7 and 8, "where I'm not happy with the coverage. I've sent two teams out to finish off that area while the other teams come back in, then I'll be sending them home. Tomorrow we are going to start to the west of Area 8 along Cypress Mountain, and to the north of Area 7 towards the Coquitlam watershed. We really don't think it's likely she could be anywhere else, based on the area we have already searched."

"Don't worry Marcel, we'll find her," he added, putting his hand on Marcel's shoulder.

Of course, he understood the safety of the crews was paramount, but it was still hard for Marcel to hear they were calling off the search for the night. They'd hope for better conditions in the morning and continue their efforts at first light. The fog and heavy rain were making things treacherous for the search crews, who had been out all day. It was getting dark and it was raining harder than ever. The pineapple express weather system was moving up from Hawaii and bringing with it a massive dump of precipitation. It would follow with warmer temperatures but those hadn't hit yet. It was cold.

Marcel took out his phone and typed out another update for his work:

"Final update for today… There was a positive sighting of her Monday at 2:30, so that helps to place where she was… but no sign of her since then. They will be shutting down soon. With this rain it is too dangerous to continue… they will be back at it at 6:30am."

Tina and Theresa followed Gerald and Marcel out of the command truck. They stood under the awning to say their goodbyes. Marcel thanked them for all their support that day. He couldn't have made it without them. He promised to keep them up to date if anything changed.

Marcel watched solemnly as the SAR teams came in off the trails. There was a heaviness in their step, there was no joy in getting to go home to their families, get fed, get warm. They wanted to find Annette too, and they were disappointed at the weather's uncooperativeness.

Before leaving, Marcel ducked back in to say, "Thanks Ian, for everything you and your team has done. I really appreciate it."

"It's our pleasure Marcel. I really thought we would find her today with the dogs and all, but sometimes things don't work out the way you expect. We'll be back up again tomorrow morning at 6:30 at the Golf and Country Club parking lot. It will be a lot more comfortable for you there. Go home and get some sleep," Ian told him.

"Thanks," Marcel replied. "Are you sure the gate will be open this time?" He asked, remembering sitting in front of the locked gate that morning.

"They say it will be… I'm pretty sure it will," Ian responded.

Gerald put his hand on Marcel's shoulder, gave it a squeeze and said, "Let's go. I'll drive."

The two men stepped into Marcel's car and Gerald started the engine. He didn't put the car in drive, they just sat there in silence. Gerald could feel what was going on and he wanted to give his little brother time to process it.

Marcel's heart was being ripped out of his chest. He was leaving his wife in the forest for another night. She needed him and there was nothing he could do to help her. He felt helpless. Hopeless.

Driving away from that base camp was the hardest thing he'd ever had to do.

The drive back to the house was quiet, sombre. Gerald pulled the car into the garage and the two men got out. Marcel's eye caught a glimpse of the vacuum cleaner hose hanging haphazardly on the wall. Annette always had trouble looping it neatly and would leave it however it happened to land on the hook. He hated it when she left it like that, but seeing it now, he felt a pang of guilt. Why had he always teased her about it? Little things like that didn't matter. If she made it home, he'd stop bugging her about it.

When she made it home.

As they entered through the back door from the garage, the house was quiet except for murmured conversation. Marcel could hear Nadine talking to Breanne and Gabrielle, probably trying to coax them to eat something. Gabrielle rose from the kitchen table when her father walked in. Marcel had texted to say he was on his way home, so she had been expecting him.

"I can't believe they didn't find her yet," Gabrielle said as she hugged her Dad.

"Me neither," replied Marcel and Gerald in unison. Gerald added, "They're doing everything they can, but this weather…"

Nadine asked if she could get anybody anything, but both men declined. Sensing they needed family time now, she and Breanne said their goodbyes and left quietly through the garage door.

Though he had no appetite, Marcel numbly busied himself with dinner preparations. He needed to keep busy, to occupy his mind and keep the bad thoughts at bay. He put the rice in the rice cooker, peeled carrots for steaming, and warmed the chicken in the oven on low. It was a quick and easy meal and one he wouldn't likely eat.

As he cooked, the rain poured down outside harder and harder. The sound went from hissing to pelting to gushing. Marcel looked fleetingly out the window and said aloud, "Please be safe!"

When dinner was ready, they gathered around the formal dining table in the dining room without much enthusiasm. They filled their plates, but no one dug in right away.

"Please try to eat something," Gabrielle urged Marcel.

"I will. I will," he replied absentmindedly.

"Dad, you've barely touched your food," complained Gabrielle.

"Yeah, come on, just eat something," chimed in Gerald. Always with the big brother act.

Marcel took a forkful of food and lifted it to his mouth. Chewing was laborious, and the food was bland. It tasted like sadness and disappointment. He had lost his flavour for food and life.

Everyone cleared the half-empty plates away, then returned to the table and sat in relative silence, a stark contrast to the pounding rain. Marcel got up twice to check for a flood in the kitchen which he was sure had occurred. Both times it was merely the rain from the upper roof falling onto the lower roof outside of the kitchen, the sound hammering and spritzing like a pipe had ruptured and was spraying water all over the kitchen.

Chloe sat on guard a few feet away, trembling. "C'mere girl," Annette invited her, and patted the ground beside her. Chloe got up and trotted to her, gave her a sniff kiss, and lay down where she was told. She lasted one or two minutes and got up again, taking her post by the tree, shivering and watching Annette.

Roxy restlessly tried to find comfort as she lay down beside a large rock, then got up, shuffled around, lay back down, only to get up again and reposition herself. Annette watched her and, though she couldn't help her much, she called her over to her and patted the ground. "Lie down, girl," she said to her sweetly. Roxy was not one to react to stern commands, but she could be sweet-talked into submission easily.

Roxy was happy to curl up with her back to Annette's left thigh. She had short hair and the cold and rain were making her shiver uncontrollably. Annette sat up with great effort and took off her blue raincoat. She took off the lighter, pink raincoat and spread it out over Roxy to give her some protection and, she hoped, a layer of warmth. She flopped onto her back and winced, realizing she had forgotten to put the blue coat back on. Ugh. She forced herself to sit back up, then pulled the coat on but didn't zip it. She lifted the hood over her head, lay down, and pulled the right side of the coat as far over to the left as she could, then folded the left side over and pulled it as far as she could to the right. Two layers of protection were better than one!

If Annette could have rolled to either side and spooned the boxer, they could have kept each other warmer, but she was in too much pain to lay on her side. Roxy licked at herself nervously.

Just when she thought it couldn't possibly rain any harder, nature said "Here, hold my beer." The rain pummeled them, and Annette felt like she was laying under a waterfall. There wasn't a single dry spot on her entire body. She took her sopping wet gloves off and blew what little breath she had into her freezing fingers. The saturated gloves only served to keep her fingers cold, so she tucked them in a pocket and pulled her sleeves over her hands. Maybe the fingers would keep each other warmer.

Annette's ears perked up. What was that sound? A banjo? How odd! Who would be playing a banjo out here in the woods in the dark on the worst night of the year? That didn't make any sense. She must be hallucinating.

Another thing that didn't make any sense was her lying in the forest for the second night in a row! Where did she go wrong? How could she be so foolish? How come she couldn't figure out which way was home?

She wiggled her toes and felt the water in her boots sploshing around her drenched socks. She had no energy to lift her leg even enough to let the water run down her leg and drain out of the boot.

Annette cried. She just wanted to go home, to have this nightmare be over. Chloe came over and gave her a whimpering kiss then went back to her spot and sat staring at her.

"It's okay girl," Annette managed between teary breaths, "we're gonna make it. They'll find us."

Her mouth and throat were hoarse and dry from yelling at the helicopters. Even in the torrential rains her lips felt chapped. She stuck her tongue out to catch some falling raindrops, but the chattering of her teeth kept her from keeping her tongue out and her mouth open. The clatter of her teeth was like a jackhammer in her head and she just wanted that sound to go away!

She had never been so cold in her entire life. Even in the Himalayan mountains, where she and her hired Sherpa climbed for weeks to the Annapurna Base Camp, she had not experienced this kind of adversity. It was cold there. This was coldest. Perhaps having dry clothes made the difference.

Annette's thoughts went to Marcel and Gabrielle. What were they doing, what were they thinking? She didn't want them to be upset; she was still breathing. "I'm alive! I'm ALIVE!!" she screamed into the night.

Chloe came to her and sat down next to her shoulder. Annette reached over and stroked her wet coat lovingly. "It's okay girl, I'm okay," she patted her. Her yelling probably startled poor Chloe. Once she made sure Annette was okay, Chloe walked back to her post.

The doorbell rang, and Gerald got up to get the door. Marcel got up too, knowing it would be his family and he was in for a hug-fest. Janette raced past Gerald with a quick, "Hi" and ran to her little brother. She put her arms around him and squeezed him, and he folded into her and burst into tears. She leaned back to look into his eyes, then stepped back, her brow knit with concern.

She put her hands on his cheeks, studied him, and asked, "How are you holding up? Have you eaten?"

"Yeah, yeah, we just had dinner," he brushed off her worry for him. There was only one person they should be worrying about right now, and she was in the forest.

"I thought you were going to stay with Dad?" Marcel questioned Janette. She told him their sister Elaine had gone to stay with their father and keep him updated.

The men followed Janette in but hung back, knowing not to get in the way of a mother bear. When Janette released him, the others came to hug Marcel.

"Good to see you!"

"How're you doing?"

"Any news?"

"I'm so sorry."

These strong, tough men, whose shoulders and strength would carry Marcel through, teared up as they hugged him.

"We had to come," said Maurice, "there was no way we could sit at home and wait."

The others nodded in agreement. This is what family meant, unwavering love and support, but an amped-up version in times of trouble. Marcel basked in their comfort.

Once settled in – coats hung up, luggage placed in bedrooms, bathroom breaks, and beverages poured - the family gathered around the dining table. Marcel had laid out the dinner leftovers in case anyone was hungry after their long drive. Most of them just held their drink glasses and picked at the food with their forks rather than taking a full plate, as families do in informal settings.

Marcel received a text from Theresa offering her parents' house in case there wasn't enough room for his family. He replied with, "Thank you, but we'll work it out." He needed them close. He felt insulated, should he crumble.

Another text offer came from a neighbour, offering spare rooms for guests. Their thoughtfulness touched Marcel, and he thanked them sincerely for their generosity. He explained kindly that he was not letting his family out of his sight, and they understood.

Marcel fixed himself a Kraken and Coke and rejoined the group at the table. He knew if he sunk into the couch, he might not be able to get back up. Gerald was telling them how they'd had to leave the mountain, how hard it had been to drive away.

"I can't believe they made you leave," scoffed Loren.

Gerald explained, "There was nothing anyone could do up there, the weather was getting too bad."

"Let's go up there anyway. We can sit in the car with our headlights on in case she walks out," Maurice suggested.

Marcel raised his eyebrows and considered this plan. "Yeah, that would be great, guys. I'd feel better if there was someone to meet her in case she did make it out."

Gerald and Andy offered to take the later shift. Maurice and Loren would leave now and return at 1:00am, then Gerald and Andy would be there from 1:30am to 6:00am. Janette would drive Marcel back to the Command Centre while the first shift slept.

With a plan in place, Marcel excused himself. He needed to lay down and rest. The alcohol had relaxed him enough to let exhaustion take hold, and he was having trouble keeping his eyes open. It was 9:00pm and he'd been awake since 7:30am the previous day. After 37 hours awake and 27 hours in a state of hyper emotions, he was drained physically and mentally.

He brushed his teeth and resented the freshness of the toothpaste. How must Annette's teeth feel right now? He didn't deserve fresh breath and clean teeth. But he went through the motions anyway, letting autopilot take him to bed. He disrobed and let the clothes fall, leaving them wherever they landed. He lifted his quilt and slid in by habit, not wanting to disturb Annette's side of the bed. He was always careful not to wake her when he got to bed late.

Marcel's eyes stung from the day's tears and the sandpaper of tiredness. He looked up at the ceiling and whispered, "Please God, bring her home. Keep her safe." And he closed his eyes and drifted away.

Tuesday, November 21st, 9:00pm

A low growl brought Annette out of her stupor. Roxy grumbled and now Chloe joined in. Roxy grunted and rose to her feet. Chloe got up from her post and paced, growling. Chloe wasn't a growler, but something was catching her attention.

Annette wasn't aware of any danger. There was no fear rising, it was buried deep beneath her survival instincts. It didn't cross her mind it could be a predator. If it had, the terror would have eaten her up. Instead, she closed her eyes against the rain.

The sound of the banjo became louder. What an odd noise to hear in the forest. Her chattering teeth hammered in her ears. The machinegun tip-tapping of the rain hitting the foliage, bouncing off logs, and dropping on her raincoat brought nothing but resentment. She was so sick of the rain, so sick of being wet.

And thirsty. Not hungry, just thirsty. The irony…

Day 3:

Wednesday,
November 22nd

He opened his eyes. He blinked as they tried to focus. His brain began waking up. An emotion seeped in. Confusion first, followed by a distant memory. Why was he so tired? His family was here. "Why are they here?" he asked his brain. "Annette was missing, they came to help," came the answer. Tears sprung into his sleep-filled eyes when he looked at her un-creased pillow. It hadn't been a nightmare. She was really missing.

He rolled onto his side and reached for her pillow. He brought it to his chest and hugged it, his body heaving with sobs. He curled himself around it and wept, not caring where the tears fell. Disbelief, denial, confusion, and desperation mixed violently in his soul and poured out in his tears.

The tears came and went, and when they had run dry, he sat on the edge of the bed and breathed deeply. It felt good to let it out, but he knew it wasn't over, there would be more.

In this moment of reprieve, he did a quick calculation and checked the time back in London, England. It was 8:00am there, and the perfect time to call Annette's Dad, Mike. He and his wife Deborah would be waiting impatiently for word of his daughter.

Marcel always left his phone charging in the kitchen, so he pulled on a pair of track pants and padded down the stairs quietly, so he wouldn't disturb the others who were hopefully getting some rest. When he reached the bottom of the stairs, he heard voices in the laundry room. He cocked his ear and listened closer. No, not the laundry room. The voices were coming from the basement.

Surprised someone was awake but glad they were because he needed company, Marcel headed to the laundry room where the door to the basement was. He expected Maurice and Loren would have just returned from their shift at the mountain and Gerald would have already left with Andy.

The conversation stopped when Marcel opened the door and started down the wooden staircase to the suite where Gerald, Maurice, and Andy were staying. When he got to the bottom of the stairs, he found not only Maurice and Loren, but also Gerald and Andy commiserating over beers. The men rose when Marcel walked in and each took a turn for a hug.

Confused, Marcel asked, "What's up? I thought you guys would be up the mountain by now."

Maurice explained, "When Loren and I got to the mountain, there was a police car there with his lights on. So we talked to him for about an hour."

Loren added, "He said there were five of them at different entrances to the mountain. They all have their lights on as a beacon in case Annette comes out."

Maurice nodded and added, "They also want to keep people off the mountain in case they try to go in and look for her themselves."

Marcel was thankful for the news. If they were stationed there expecting her to come walking out, they hadn't given up on her. There was still hope.

They sat and talked for a while longer but by 2:30am, everyone was starting to fade. Marcel bid them all good night and headed upstairs to get his phone.

Once back in his bedroom, he sat on the edge of the bed and called Mike and Deborah in London. Mike was the jovial sort, always joking around when he spoke to Marcel, but this time he couldn't have been more serious. He and Deborah were beside themselves with worry.

"I've got a friend who works at St. Paul's Cathedral here in London and they're all saying prayers for Annette," Mike relayed. Marcel was warmed by this news, appreciating every positive thought from around the globe. It felt good to talk to Mike and Deborah, people who loved Annette as much as he did. Sharing grief was a closeness you could only have with true family.

Marcel promised to call them as soon as he had news and disconnected. After half an hour of talking, there wasn't much left to say. All they could do was hope and pray.

He looked at the digital clock on the nightstand. It glowed 3:00am. In three hours, it would all start again. The searching, the waiting, the worrying. Suddenly the emotions flooded in again.

Marcel cupped his hand over his mouth to stave off the scream that welled inside him. Tears streamed from his eyes and pooled where his fingers gripped his cheek. He didn't know if he could make it through another day like yesterday.

"They'll find her," screamed his heart.

"But what if they don't," retaliated his head. "What will happen if she never comes back? What will you do? Will you sell the house? Will you buy a new car?"

Marcel was shocked at the thoughts running through his mind in this, his darkest hour. How could he think such things? Where was his mind taking him? Sanity had clearly left him.

He slid to the floor, leaned against the bed and hugged his knees. He let out a silent scream and cried harder.

"This can't be happening," he told himself.

"But it is," said the devil inside. "She's gone forever!"

Would he ever see Chloe again? He wanted her cold nose and puppy snuggles now more than ever.

Shattered, Marcel pulled himself up and into the bed. And he wept.

He wanted time to go faster so it would be daylight and the search would resume. But time seemed to stand still, and hours passed between his breaths as he gasped through tears. The last time he dared look at the clock, the lit numbers beamed 5:15.

Marcel blinked. His eyes were puffy from the previous hours of torment. He braced for another flood of desperation, but it didn't come. Instead, he woke up calm. Still. Hopeful. Tears had washed away the negativity and anguish. The darkness in his soul had dissipated and hope blossomed where despair once lived.

For the first time in what felt like weeks, his heart was full of hope instead of dread.

Marcel reached up and turned off the alarm clock which was set for 6:00am. He was ready to get on with the day. THIS was the day Annette was coming home. Neither dream nor premonition told him so, only he could feel it in his bones. Today was the day.

After a quick shower, Marcel tiptoed down the stairs to the kitchen to find his sister Janette waiting for him.

"Good morning," she whispered, not wanting to wake the others.

"It is," said Marcel as he kissed his sister on the head and gave her a big hug. Then said with determination, "That's enough of this shit. Let's go bring her home!"

They found the gate to the Country Club open when they arrived, so they pulled into the lot and parked where they could see the SAR truck. The lot was large and had plenty of room for the Command Centre, the news crews, the volunteers, and anyone who wanted to come support the family and searchers. Marcel and Janette sat in the car and watched as everyone prepared for the day, the SAR teams converging to their right and the news teams setting up equipment to their left. It looked like an epic battle was about to take place between two armies, even though everyone was on the same team.

Though he was certain Annette would be found today, Marcel formulated what he wanted to tell the news crews. He didn't want people to give up, to stop believing she'd be found alive. He needed to get the message out that she WAS going to be found safe and sound. He believed it. He wanted them to believe it too.

The rain persisted but had lightened, now more of an ever-present misty rain rather than the large hard drops from the night before. It brought with it a dense fog which sat below the mountain. They had driven through it to get to the country club. This meant the helicopters would be able to fly above the trees. The misty rain and fog looked eerie in the dim light of the morning but wouldn't hold back the operations.

Around 7:00am, the search teams formed a half circle outside the Command Truck to receive their final instructions from the SAR Manager, a man Marcel didn't recognize. Marcel and Janette joined them at the back, wanting to hear what they were being told. He also wanted to say something to them before they headed out into the bush.

"Some of you have long assignments, some of you have shorter ones. Just the luck of the draw folks," the SAR Manager said loudly so everyone could hear him. "When you've completed your assignment, come back, eat, warm up, and we might send you out again," he continued.

Once the manager was finished and the group started to break up and make their way to their transport to the mountain, Marcel grabbed the opportunity to talk. "One more thing," Marcel said as he raised his hand. Everyone turned to look at who was addressing them.

The SAR Manager yelled out, "Folks, this is Victor, Annette's husband."

Marcel paused, unsure if the man was talking about him. Was that some sort of code name for the aggrieved husband?

Everyone looked at him expectantly. Marcel tried to speak but the words were getting caught in his throat. He struggled to get the words out without breaking down, and finally managed to say, "I just wanted to say thank you." He gulped, and pushed out, "Be careful out there," before his words faltered. These were the people that were going out into that horrible weather on their own time to find his wife. This was the least he could say to let them know how much they and their actions meant to him.

A man with a dark beard approached Marcel, gave him a hug and said, "Don't worry, my brother. We'll find her." Marcel marvelled at the never-ending warmth and positivity these searchers conveyed. It bolstered his belief Annette would be home by the end of the day.

Wednesday, November 22nd, 7:20am

As the dawn chased away the dark, it did not bring with it determination. Annette was spent. She admitted to herself she could not get up again. She lay still, shivering. Roxy lay curled up against her, licking herself constantly, the raincoat covering her. Bubba lay under the fern, Chloe sat upright at her post. Annette doubted if Chloe had gotten a wink of sleep. She herself hadn't gotten much, fading in and out of consciousness. With the darkness, it was hard to tell if her eyes were open or if she had fallen asleep.

Daylight brought little relief. The rain didn't let up, and Annette was freezing. Since she knew there was no hope she could find her way out, crawling or otherwise, she resigned herself to laying in wait. Rescue was her only option for getting out of that bush alive.

Even though she'd been in the same spot all night, she couldn't move. She lay there for what felt like eternity.

Marcel wanted to address the news crews once he had regained his composure. As he crossed the parking lot heading for their tent, he crossed paths with a gorgeous Belgian Malinois Search and Rescue dog.

Marcel, desperate for doggy cuddles, asked the dog's handler, "Can I say hello to your dog?"

"Of course! She's very friendly," the woman replied.

That was an understatement. The dog leaned into Marcel as he scratched her neck. She rubbed up against his legs and gave him all the love she had. It was wonderful.

"What's her name?" he asked the woman.

"Her name is Envy," said the woman. Marcel offered his hand and introduced himself. "I'm Kira, one of the Surrey SAR team members," she responded as she shook his hand.

Marcel knelt down to hug Envy, and whispered in her ear, "Help us find Annette." The dog licked his face in reply and wriggled out of his grasp, as if in a hurry to get out there and make that promise come true! It was amazing how animals helped to ease the burden of life and lift your spirits, and the interaction with Envy was just what Marcel had needed.

Empowered by the dog encounter, Marcel headed for the news crews. He needed to tell them more about Annette, about her strength and courage and stubbornness. She was capable of surviving this and she deserved to be saved.

They saw him approaching and scrambled to get their gear ready. Marcel recognized a few of them by now – Susie from CBC and Jordan from Global – and he was feeling more comfortable with answering questions in the face of a camera. Before they turned their cameras on, Marcel told them he wanted to focus on what kind of a person Annette was. *Is*.

"How are you holding up today, sir?" someone asked.

"Today is good. Today is going to be a good day," Marcel replied confidently.

Another reporter agreed, "It feels right, doesn't it?"

Marcel, delighted at the positivity, replied, "It does, you know. It was awful last night, the rain, the cold yesterday. But today it's, you know, it looks like it's holding off a little bit, and um, I think it's going to be a good day today." He nodded for emphasis.

One reporter remarked, "I think you're right. It's 14 degrees right now, so that's best for everybody."

Marcel agreed.

"How did you sleep last night?" someone else asked.

Marcel told them he hadn't slept the first night but managed to catch a few winks that night.

Then came the opportunity he'd been waiting for! A reporter asked Marcel, "Can you tell me a little bit about your wife?"

"I would love to," Marcel brightened.

"What is she like as a person?" the reporter continued. This was exactly what Marcel had been hoping to relay to them. He wanted them to know who she was, what she stood for, what kind of heart she had.

Marcel shook his head and started, "Oh boy. Just after I met her, she packed her backpack and she went to India for three months! She's 4 foot 11, blond hair, and was by herself for 3 months. She took trains and busses to Katmandu, hired a trecker there and hiked for two weeks up to the Annapurna base camp."

"Then she hiked back down and traveled through the south of India. She knows how to take care of herself," Marcel said proudly.

"Yeah, that sounds promising," encouraged a reporter.

Marcel carried on without prompting, "Yes, she loves animals. She's rescued every kind of animal we have here: racoons, cats, dogs. She tried rescuing a coyote once, thinking it was a dog. That was a bit exciting." Everyone laughed.

"She rescued a teenager off the street just a couple of years ag; she brought her into our home. It didn't work out exactly as she had hoped, but the girl is doing better. Basically, with love, she taught her how to live." Marcel beamed with pride, thinking about what a big heart Annette had, and how lucky he was to have married such a warm and caring soul.

"How long have you been married?" asked someone.

Marcel answered without hesitation, "22 years now."

"When you see all these volunteers here, what goes through your mind?" asked a different reporter.

Marcel gushed, "Oh my God, these guys are the greatest. I can't say enough about them. They are doing amazing work, they're the best. They have passion. They know what they are doing, they are doing what they can and…" He shrugged.

"Do you have hope?" asked one.

His resolve was strong, but his voice started to waver when he replied, "Absolutely. You know what? This is… it's time to wrap things up, go home. It's time to bring Annette home. She deserves it, you know? She deserves it, she's capable. She's out there. We are going to bring her home."

A gentleman approached Marcel and Janette as they stood watching the workers get on with their day.

"Hi Marcel, I'm Dario," he introduced himself as he stuck out his hand. Marcel shook it and cocked his head expectantly.

"I'm a SAR member and my primary job today is to keep you informed and make you comfortable. If you need anything, let me know and I'll do my best to help you out," he offered.

"Wow, that's very kind," Marcel replied, not feeling as if he was deserving of any coddling but grateful to have someone with him who could answer his questions.

They chatted briefly about the Command Truck, about the searchers, and about the helicopters, which they hoped would be able to fly out in the next few hours. Marcel had no pressing needs at this point, but it was good to know there was help if he needed it.

"The Golf Club has a private room inside if you want or need some privacy. There are also washrooms inside and you're welcome to use them," he spoke to both Marcel and Janette. They nodded their thanks, but neither made a move toward the Club. Neither wanted to sit in a room and stare at the walls. Standing outside felt right.

Once Dario walked away, Marcel jerked his head sideways at Janette and led her to the covered unloading area of the Club. They were still outside and could see the activity, but at least they were dry and out of the way.

Nadine and her husband, Gerald, showed up, Gerald sporting his outdoor gear and ready to hit the trails looking for Annette. Marcel discouraged him, saying, "We have to leave this to the professionals." Gerald nodded in disappointed agreement, and the four stood under the roof of the Club and watched the news crews. The searchers had all gone to their assignments, so aside from each other, there wasn't much to look at.

Ten minutes later, the rest of Marcel's family showed up. All four men hugged Marcel then shook hands with Nadine and Gerald. Everyone echoed Annette would be found today. Whether they believed it or not didn't matter, but Marcel had no doubt in his mind.

As the family and friends stood around, some praying and others consoling, they heard the thwapping sound of the helicopter's blades nearby. It gave them a grain of hope.

The sound of helicopter in the distance brought her to full wakefulness. She cupped her hand to her ear to hear which direction they were coming from. They were still looking for her! Why couldn't they SEE her?! She was waving the damned pink raincoat! How many pink things did they see in the forest, for crying out loud?!

They must not be able to see her, she concluded. She would have to find a clearing where she would be more visible. That would require moving, something she didn't think she could do. But when push came to shove, and something needed to be done, Annette was never one to give up trying.

"Okay, Roxy. I need you to move now, okay," she urged, and gave Roxy's rear a little pat. Roxy stopped licking and looked at her sadly. "C'mon, move it! We need to get outta here," she prodded.

Roxy got up, sliding the raincoat to the ground. She walked a few feet, then turned around to see what Annette was doing.

From her vantage point on the ground, Annette could only see to her left and straight above her. The log she was lying beside blocked her view in the other direction. There seemed to be some sort of clearing in the distance, but she would have to stand up to make sure there wasn't a closer one.

She raised her right knee and wedged her foot between the ground and the log she lay beside. She pushed and thrust her body to her left side. Daggers shot through her left hip and ribcage, the muscles spasming, and she screamed in pain. She used the momentum to roll fully forward, onto her stomach, in preparation for getting upright. With her elbows tucked under her, ready to lever her trunk up, she pulled her right knee under her and pushed herself up to kneeling.

Roxy whined as she watched Annette. Bubba came out of his den, and Chloe stood at the ready. "Okay, guys, we have to get moving. Let's go," she said as she pulled herself up for what she knew would be the last time. It was harder than anything she'd ever had to do, and she was sure she couldn't do it again.

Her legs trembled, and she reached for a tree to steady herself. Annette looked around her and, spotting what she thought to be a clearing nearby, she pointed her body in that direction. After a few steps, her legs wobbled and a yelp escaped her as she crumbled forward to the forest floor. Her once-sturdy legs were no longer strong enough to carry her.

If her legs couldn't do it, her arms would have to step up. Annette was on her hands and knees, crawling slowly but making some progress to her destination, the place she hoped the canopy had a big enough gap for the helicopters to see her pink jacket.

Ten feet. That's as far as she got before she heard the whup whup return. She turned her face skyward to hear which direction it flew. It was coming fast so she quickly grabbed a stick and laid on her side to drape the coat over the end. She waved the stick in the air with both hands, working through the burning pain in her side. The helicopter circled widely but didn't come directly over her. She watched it as it lazily droned above the canopy, weaving in and out of her line of sight.

"I'm over here," she hollered hoarsely. Her throat was dry and raw from the previous day's yelling, so it was barely a rasp now. They didn't hear her. They didn't see her. The helicopter banked to the right and flew away.

Panic set in. Annette began to cry as she dropped her head back onto the twigs and leaves. They were never going to find her. They might even stop looking! She prayed with all her might, like she'd never prayed before in her life. Never a church-goer, she'd always been more of an agnostic in adulthood. But now, she needed faith. She needed to pray.

"Please God, let them find me! Why can't they see me? I need your help," she pleaded.

"If there's anything you need…" was a common thread in every communication of the past 40 hours. Marcel's friend Brian called him to offer support. Friends Sandy and Jennifer arrived to offer their services and met with hugs and tears and 'they'll find her's. Another shining light in the gloom was Icy, a young Siberian Husky client of Annette's. Icy had lived with them for a month while his owners were away, so Marcel had a special bond with the young dog. He showed up with his owner who, like all Annette's clients, had become not only a client but a friend.

Marcel knelt down to say hello to Icy, and the husky sat back on her haunches and popped her paws up onto Marcel's shoulders. She covered Marcel in kisses, and each time Marcel tried to divide his attention by looking at someone else, Icy would put her face right in front of his so they would maintain eye contact. There was nothing like puppy love. Few things could compare in times of stress for calming the nerves.

Annette's friend Susan, someone who often joined Annette on her walks, arrived with a container of warm dumplings for everyone. She had seen Marcel on the morning news so knew exactly where to find him.

"Let's go inside to eat," suggested Janette. "They said we could go inside, right Marcel?"

Marcel nodded and followed the others inside. He didn't have an appetite and wouldn't likely eat anything, but it would be nice to sit down for a while. Pangs of guilt waved through him as he thought about Annette, and how cold she must be. And hungry. Was she hungry?

Inside the lobby was a large sitting area with a few couches and chairs, enough for everyone to sit comfortably. Susan put the container of dumplings on the large coffee table and a few people leaned forward to grab one with their fingers.

"I hate just sitting here doing nothing," Andy huffed. "Is there something else we could be doing that might help?" he looked at Gerald, expecting the ex-RCMP officer to have some suggestions.

Gerald thought for a few minutes while he chewed on a dumpling. Two dumplings later, he shared some ideas.

"Oh, I like the idea of putting up flyers," Maurice exclaimed. "One of the dogs may have been spotted wandering around a neighbourhood!"

"Or maybe even Annette, if she's disoriented…" chimed Loren.

The men decided to get posters made and put them up in all the communities surrounding the mountain. Marcel texted Gerald pictures of Annette and the dogs, and Gerald left immediately, headed for the print shop to have the posters made. Everyone was satisfied to have at least some kind of contribution to the search. Moral support was great, but truly helping felt good.

While Gerald went off on his errand, the group waited impatiently. They lobbed some small talk and shed occasional tears, then contained themselves and settled back into their holding pattern.

Wednesday, November 22nd, 9:55am

Annette lifted her eyes skyward. She lay on her back and let the rain hit her face, not caring to wipe it away. She was numb, both physically and mentally. Every ounce of energy and hope had drained from her body, and she was finished.

Time was meaningless. She had no idea what time of day it was, and it didn't matter. Nothing mattered anymore. The hours dragged on and Annette thought nightfall was imminent. She knew she wouldn't survive another night out there. Her body was broken. Her spirit was broken.

"I've had a good life," she thought to herself. There was no point in having regrets or wishing wishes, it was over. It was time to accept her fate and stop fighting. She knew Marcel and Gabrielle would be fine, they could take care of themselves. She felt sorry for the dogs and hoped they could find their way out. They were not moving yet, though, and sat blinking at Annette, waiting for her next move.

Acceptance and peace blanketed Annette. She was ready to let go. She didn't feel scared or angry. She didn't hear the wind in the trees or the rain or the dogs. Peace and quiet. Annette was calm. She closed her eyes and waited for whatever life she had left to drain out of her.

Marcel's phone rang in his pocket. The call display showed Gabrielle. "Here we go again," Marcel thought, "another morning when I need to break the bad news to her." But this morning was different. He knew she would be found today. Now he just had to give Gabrielle that confidence too!

"Good morning, sweetie," he answered, which was how he usually answered her morning phone calls.

"Good morning, Dad. Any news?" she asked eagerly.

"I'm sorry, sweetheart, nothing yet. There are even more search crews out today. They will find her soon. I know they will!" he asserted.

"Ok, Dad," she sighed. He could hear the pain in her voice.

"Sweetie, they *will* find her today," Marcel assured her." You know Mom, she is too stubborn to let that mountain beat her! She's strong…. you know that. They will find her!"

"I know, Dad," she replied, unconvinced but appeasing him.

"Somebody will be down soon, I don't want you to be alone," he said with concern. "Nadine, would you mind going back to the house and keeping an eye on Gabrielle?" Marcel asked.

Nadine stood up and took her car keys out of her pocket in reply. "Tell her I'll be there in four minutes," she said as she scooted past the others on the couch. Nadine's husband Gerald stayed behind to be on hand in case Marcel needed anything.

Twenty minutes later, another friendly face showed up.

"There you are," said Stuart as he walked into the Country Club. "I brought backup!" He introduced Marcel to another man fully decked out in outdoor gear. These men were ready for battle in the bush! Excited to have someone whose searching he could direct, Stuart laid out a map on the table and Marcel showed them the search areas.

"They've already searched these areas," he said as he outlined with his finger on the map. "And today they're doing these areas," he swept his finger to the north of the powerline. "Can you guys go check in this corner over here?" indicating a northern area between the mountain and Coquitlam Lake, where the town's drinking water came from.

As the men huddled over the map, another man with a familiar face Marcel couldn't place, walked in. He walked purposefully to Marcel and the Mayor of Coquitlam, Richard Stewart, introduced himself.

"I'm sorry you're having to deal with this terrible time. Is there anything I can do for you or your family?" he asked with genuine concern.

"I don't think there's anything we need at the moment, thanks," replied Marcel. "There's not much we can do."

Maurice, who worked for the City of Kelowna, shared with the Mayor how the Kelowna City crews helped out in the summer when the surrounding hillsides were rife with wildfires.

"We were out there on the roads anyway, so we kept an eye out for fires, hotspots, wildlife, lost pets, or anything else people needed. We even posted flyers," he explained helpfully.

The Mayor nodded politely and took the advice cordially. He then smiled, seemingly to himself, and wandered over to look at the map with the others. He was not there for the publicity, though the news crews would want to interview him; he was there out of a sincere desire to help.

But he had a secret.

Roxy growled with more intensity than during the night. Annette looked in Roxy's direction and saw her ears perked, staring into the forest from where she lay. "What is it Roxy? Why are you growling?" Annette asked meekly. She felt no fear, no fight or flight instinct. Nothing could move her from this, her final resting place.

On her feet now, Roxy began to bark. Not simply warning barks, these were barks of alarm. Bubba joined in and started to howl, her bark more of an "arooooo" than a "woof."

A single, faint whistle pierced the silence between Roxy's barks. Another banjo? It couldn't be, because this time Roxy heard it too! She kept barking, and Annette knew something, or someone, was approaching.

"I'm over here! I'm over here," Annette strained her voice to yell above the barking.

When the words, "We're coming," reached Annette's ears, tears sprung to her eyes. In a final release of all her pent-up anger and pain, she cried. It was unbelievable, but someone had found her! "It's going to take us a little while to get to you, but we'll be there," the man's voice called to her.

"She won't bite, she's just being protective," Annette squeaked, hoping her rescuer could hear her. "Roxy, come here, girl," she coaxed. No, Roxy would not be swayed. She stood at attention and barked at the intruder.

It took some time for the man to make his way over the debris, large and slippery logs blocking his access at every step. Annette heard his radio chirp as he reported he'd made contact with the subject.

"Hi Annette," he called as he trudged, "I'm Darren and I'll be your host for this evening." Just what she needed, a jokester. Annette laughed through her tears.

When he got near, Darren, a very tall, fit man, dropped his backpack and took out a protein bar. Though she assured him Roxy would not bite, he kept his distance. "The other team members are coming in, so I'm going to try to get the dog to stop barking. Is it okay if I give her some granola bar?" he asked Annette.

"Okay," was all she could manage. She desperately wanted him to come help her, but there was nothing she could do to help with the dog.

He tore off pieces of the snack bar and tossed them at Roxy. She ignored them and continued to sound the alarm as she guarded Annette. To no one's surprise, Bubba dove in and hoovered up every bit of granola he could find. A few minutes later, other team members joined them, and Roxy finally calmed down, sensing there was no danger to Annette.

Annette noticed how much mud covered each of her rescuers, none of them sporting anything clean or dry from the waist down. She didn't remember it being that muddy when she laid down last night, but the torrential downpour during the night must have made the ground around her a sopping, boggy mess. The team immediately sprang into action, each knowing exactly what their job was and how to do it efficiently.

An orange, dome tarp about 3' wide x 3' high x 5' long was set up above her. It seemed to pop up by itself, because one minute it wasn't there and the next minute it was. Everyone huddled under it while they tended to her and completed their tasks. One SAR member set up a camping stove and began to make hot chocolate for Annette. Another member somehow managed to get a board (or was it a tarp?) underneath her. They took turns trying to find her pulse, but she was so close to hypothermic, it was eluding them altogether.

"Can you tell me where you're hurt?" asked a man with a thick, red beard who had introduced himself as Aidon.

"My left side," Annette said as she tried to point to it. Her arms were too heavy to move.

"Do you know what day it is?" another person asked.

Annette tried to think back to when she started the hike. "It's Wednesday," she answered.

"Do you know what time it is?" asked someone. "I dunno. Dinnertime?" Annette suggested.

"Do you have your period?" asked the female SAR member. Annette did a mental eyeroll and said, "No, I'm in menopause."

"Sorry, we have to ask all these questions," the girl said apologetically.

"Have you drunk anything?" one asked. "No, I tried to get some rain with my tongue but I couldn't," she replied. "Didn't you hear that creek running beside you?" the man asked her with surprise. "What creek?" was her reply.

The female rescuer tried to remove Annette's clothing, but it was stuck to her skin like glue, and if she tried to move Annette's limbs, Annette yelped in pain. "Is it okay if we cut your clothes off?" she asked.

"Go for it," Annette encouraged. She was in no position to be shy. Somehow, they got dry clothes onto her body without too many complaints from her. Then they lay Hot Pockets, little packets of heat activated by pressing on them, along her legs and arms. They snugged blankets and sleeping bags around her and trussed her up like a mummy.

When the hot chocolate was ready, they put it into a water bottle. Unable to lift her head to drink it, Annette held it on her chest for warmth. One of the searchers said to another, "Next time we go out, make sure everyone has a straw!" Annette was impressed by how they used every search as a learning experience.

As they fussed over her and bustled about, Annette felt a sense of relief and gratitude like she had never felt before. She was always the one to take care of everyone, and now someone was taking care of her! She felt like a baby bird, tucked under the wing of a mama bird. Safe. Secure. Protected. Saved!

"Thank you, guys. Thank you so much. You are my angels," Annette repeated over and over. The SAR team smiled at her, elated to have a good outcome to their three-day search.

RCMP Corporal Mike McLaughlin walked into the Club and invited Marcel over to him with a wave. "We need some place private we can talk," he said quietly, not wanting to be overheard by the others on the couches.

At first, Marcel wasn't surprised, as the RCMP had periodically come by to ask more questions about Annette. But as the officer looked for a private place, Marcel began to tremble. Anticipation, fear, anxiety, shock, tiredness, emotion, all of it shook through him. Was this the news he'd been waiting to hear? Corporal Mike led him down some stairs into another seating area, away from the other people but still within their line of sight. He sat down in a chair, so Marcel sat on the couch closest to him.

Cpl Mike looked at Marcel and said gently, "They found her."

Marcel exhaled, not realizing he'd been holding his breath. His chest heaved as he tried to inhale, the news knocking the wind from his lungs. His eyes welled up and a river of tears ran down his face. The swiftness of his emotional release was unexpected, but he didn't try to stop it. He could see his family and friends watching him closely, knowing he was getting news but unsure of the circumstances.

In disbelief, he asked Cpl Mike if she was okay.

"Yes, she's okay. She's responding well but she's hurt her back," he reported.

Marcel gasped for breath as he tried to find the words. Instead he gave his supporters a thumbs-up. He could hear the Club erupt into cheers as he leaned forward, pressed his forehead into his hand and cried happy tears. His girl was coming home, just as he knew she would.

Marcel pulled himself together and took out his phone as he headed up the stairs. His first call needed to be to Gabrielle, but when he gave her the news, she already knew!

"Gerald called and told Nadine," Gabrielle exclaimed. "I'm coming up there, Dad! I want to see her!"

Marcel disconnected and looked at Nadine's husband, Gerald, in surprise. "How did you know?" he asked him incredulously.

"When the Mayor was here talking to you, he already knew, but he wanted to let the RCMP give you the news. They have to give out so much bad news, he owed it to them to let them have this. While Corporal Mike was telling you, the Mayor was telling everyone around him,"

Gerald explained.

Next, Marcel dialled his father in Kelowna. His father was overcome with emotion, and Marcel was glad his sister Elaine was there to comfort him.

After he hung up, Marcel received a call from Jordan Amstrong, a member of the Global News team. Marcel shared the good news and Jordan burst into tears. Marcel was touched by his compassion and empathy, reaffirming his belief Jordan was good people.

London was the next place he called. The shriek of raw emotion skewered Marcel's ear and filled his heart as he heard pure joy in Deborah and Mike's voices.

After hugging everyone in the Club, Marcel went out to thank whoever was in the SAR truck. He didn't know what the protocol was for addressing people who had the power and ability to bring people home and rebuild families, but he hoped endless hugs and thank-yous would begin to show how much he appreciated them making his life whole again.

The managers and SAR members present filed out of the truck to greet him in the parking lot. There were ear-to-ear grins, much back-slapping and hand shaking and clapping as everyone celebrated the triumph.

"Marcel, here's what's happening now," the manager announced. "The search crew is putting Annette into a stabilizing brace that she will lay in for a long line rescue by the search helicopter."

"Really? She is going to be dangling under a helicopter? She won't like that too much," Marcel said, knowing how afraid of heights she was.

"She will be bundled up pretty tight, and there will be someone on either side of her to make sure she is safe," the SAR manager explained. "She is in good spirits, actually, really good spirits, considering what she went through," he sounded surprised. "They think she has hurt her back, but don't know for sure how severe it is. They will just make sure she is bundled tight so there isn't any further damage."

"The helicopter has landed on the golf course over that small hill there," he said pointing to the north east of where they were standing. "They are attaching the long line and making sure they have everything they need and everything is safety tested. Once the helicopter lifts off again, it will take about 25 minutes to fly over to where she is, drop the line down, hook Annette and the search crew accompanying her to the line, then fly back to here. At that point, they will get her into the ambulance and do some further testing to try to determine the scope and severity of her injuries. Then the ambulance will pull up to where you will be, and you can join her."

"I get to ride in the ambulance with her then?" Marcel asked, excited at the thought of seeing her again.

"Things will depend a lot on how she is doing. If she is stable, there is no reason why you can't ride in with her. Your daughter will likely have to ride up front with the driver. If the paramedics feel there is no danger, they may even let her ride in the back with you," he said.

"Thank you so much for everything you've done. I can't say it enough… thank you," Marcel said to him, then gave the manager a hug.

Marcel noticed Gabrielle had shown up, but was staying to one side, hoping to avoid the limelight. As he broke from the crowd and walked toward her, the camera crew rushed over to get footage of their emotional first meeting. Nadine and Janette were having none of it, and positioned themselves between Gabrielle and the camera. Gabrielle was an extremely private person, and these Mama Bears were ready to protect her privacy!

"I'll come see you guys for an interview at the tent in a few minutes, okay?" Marcel offered as he waved away the cameras. They obliged and focused their aim at others in the lot. The crowd of family, friends, SAR members, the Mayor, firemen, all made for good copy.

Gabrielle fell into her father's embrace and the two shared tears of relief and elation.

"She's coming home," Marcel said into her hair as he held her.

"I know, Dad, just like you said she would," Gabrielle beamed as she hugged him harder. Nadine came, touched Gabrielle's arm, and suggested, "Let's go into the Club so we can wait for your Mom in private."

The two walked away and Marcel turned to the news crews, anxiously waiting behind the ribbon holding them back. True to his word, he walked over to their tent, ready to answer anything they threw at him.

The first question was, "Marcel, you knew they were going to find her today. How did you know?"

Marcel thought for a moment, then answered from his heart, "Faith! Some things just don't need an explanation for." In the back of his mind he was thinking *faith in Annette's ability to survive, faith in the search crews to do what they train so hard for, faith in God…*

"What did it feel like when you heard the news?" was the next question.

"I couldn't breathe. It was just amazing. The RCMP officer came to talk to me and you just can't imagine what that feels like. I've had some dark days here. I woke up this morning and I just," Marcel said, strength in his voice for the first time in days, shaking his fist, "I just knew it, I knew she was coming home today." He paused and looked over his shoulder at the helicopter flying overhead. "That's why I came and talked to you this morning."

"You knew it, didn't you?" the reporter repeated.

"I knew it. I knew it, and it happened. I wish someone had asked me what time because I would have told you 11:00, and I would have gotten it right. Logic told me by the time they grouped in the morning, got their Search Area, made their way out to that area and had some time to start searching, it was going to be 11:00 when they found her."

"What do you think of the Search and Rescue volunteers?" asked another reporter.

The people who are here today, obviously I am amazed at the type of work they do. The people here are just incredible, who have been out there searching day and night," Marcel gushed. "When you are in a situation, the mind is a dangerous thing. It goes into all sorts of dark holes, and suddenly that all just disappears. You just, you know, there is light… an incredible amount of love," Marcel shrugged, searching for the right words to describe the emotions.

"The support," he continued, "all the people who have come from out of town to support us, all the messages I am getting… my pocket is just vibrating right now with all the messages I'm getting. To all those people, I'm sorry if I didn't get back to you, but trust me, I appreciate them, and I'll read them. She's coming home," Marcel declared.

Marcel thanked the SAR for their hard work, dedication, professionalism, compassion and their passion for their job.

"These people are volunteers who left their families and their jobs to come find Annette. I cannot possibly say enough. This is the result they work for; this is their reward. They made it themselves and they deserve everything they can get," he spoke from the heart. "Support your local Search and Rescue, and you know what? Hug your spouse tonight. Whoever you're lying in bed with tonight, hold on to them."

Then came the question he had been expecting, "What are you going to say when you see her?"

"Oh my God. I'm not sure we will be talking much," Marcel replied with a grin, "but I told our daughter we will wait till we get home before we start giving her shit!"

Remembering the cameras were rolling, he covered his mouth and impishly said, "Oops! Sorry!"

"That's ok," a few of the reporters said, completely understanding the raw emotions Marcel was feeling.

"Let's clear away some of these sticks so we have room for the stretcher," Darren told the others. Every time someone threw a stick into the forest, Chloe retrieved it. She was a Border Collie; that was her *job*! Everyone laughed, and to Annette, the levity was welcome.

Bubba knew what was what and curled up next to Annette's shoulder and promptly fell asleep, finally out of the rain. The safety and comfort of the shelter allowed him to fully relax after days of restless dozing.

Roxy, too, got herself out of the rain and lay under the tarp canopy. Annette thought Roxy had probably fared the worst, as her short hair didn't keep her warm or dry. Her nervous licking had stopped now that there was activity to keep her attention.

The SAR team got to work cutting down smaller trees in an effort to make room for the helicopter.

"You mean, they can land the helicopter here?" Annette asked in astonishment.

"Ha, ha. No," replied Darren. "They're going to lower the long line and lift you out of here in the stretcher!"

Annette's spunkiness returned, and she said, "No way!" She was terrified of heights and there was no way she was going to be dangling below a helicopter above the trees! Nope, nope, nope. She shook her head, but it was more of a tremor than a shake.

They ignored her protests and picked up the stretcher holding her, looked at each other and chuckled. "I guess we don't need six people to lift you," someone laughed. "We train with 200-pound men as subjects!"

"How are the dogs getting out?" asked Annette as they lowered her to the ground where the longline would be hooked up. She was more worried about them than herself.

They informed her the dogs would be longlined out after she was transported. She begged them to take the dogs first, but they wouldn't hear of it. "Don't worry, we'll take care of the dogs," they assured her.

"I'm so scared of heights," Annette whimpered.

"Gotcha," said Aidon, and he put a pair of goggles over her eyes and pulled the blanket over her head like a big hood. "There! Now you won't see a thing," he proclaimed.

Annette felt like a swaddled baby, and it felt great! Someone rubbed her hands to warm them while they waited for the helicopter to arrive, which seemed to take forever. She was too excited to relax or sleep, excited to see Marcel and Gabrielle, to sleep in her own bed, to live life again. She had a second chance!

Though she couldn't see them, she could hear the SAR members talking to each other, complaining about a news helicopter which was circling. They radioed someone to "Get that chopper out of here!"

When the rescue helicopter neared, they put hearing protection over her ears, and Annette held her breath.

"Are you okay?" a voice asked loudly.

"I'm okay," she yelled, thinking they couldn't hear her very well with all the noise. She was okay. She was scared to death, but she wasn't dead. She was ALIVE!

Annette felt the longline being hooked onto the stretcher, and suddenly she felt like she was floating up. She concentrated on the sound of the helicopter, praying the sound didn't change so she would know she was safe. When she was lowered to the ground, she didn't feel a thing, only that the floating sensation had stopped.

There was cheering in the distance, and Annette wondered what was going on because she still couldn't see anything. She could tell the stretcher was lifted up onto a gurney, then the stretcher was pulled out from under her. They wheeled her somewhere, and suddenly she was in an ambulance. The paramedic had a lot of questions…

An ambulance crew arrived and touched base with the SAR manager. They needed to know the approximate time of arrival as well as Annette's condition, in order to prepare for her transport to the hospital.

Marcel stood with them, listening for any updates. He heard she was speaking and in good spirits.

"Yeah, she would be," Marcel chuckled.

The paramedic spoke directly to Marcel, "We'll have to assess her first, and if she's stable, you and your daughter can both ride in the back on the way to the hospital. If she's not, your daughter will have to ride in the front."

Marcel nodded, completely understanding they needed to stay out of the way while Annette was being tended to.

The search teams started returning to the base and Marcel greeted each of them as they arrived. Their once-professional demeanours turned to hugs, tears, backslaps, joy, and laughter. There weren't enough words to thank them. There would never be enough words.

Gabrielle, anxious to see her mother, ventured to the roadside near where the helicopter would land. The press was too close for her comfort, so the firemen offered Gabrielle and Nadine the cab of their firetruck to sit in while they waited. Marcel joined them presently, and it felt good to be grounded and out of the public eye for a few moments.

Marcel hopped out of the firetruck when he saw a group of work friends approaching. Tracy, Ray, Lawrence and two Brians showed up to much happier circumstances than when they had left the office an hour before. They had come to console him but instead, they got to rejoice!

They all watched as the helicopter lifted off and the rope swung into line behind it. They were going to get her! Finally, this nightmare would end!

Marcel's brothers Gerald and Andy flanked Marcel, and the threesome stood with their arms around each other. The weight of the world had lifted off their shoulders and lightness carried them. They joked around, smiled for pictures, and remarked, "There wasn't enough good news in this world lately!"

A reporter asked Marcel if he was going to grill her, and Gerald snapped back, "The grilling is going to come from her! We are going to get the grilling. 'You guys, what took you so long?!'" They all guffawed, knowing that was exactly what Annette would say.

They watched breathlessly as the helicopter flew back with its tightly wound package floating 100 feet below the chopper. "Boy, she won't like that," said one brother, knowing Annette was acrophobic. Another remarked, "Wish I could do that!" Someone replied, "You mean, fly a helicopter? Or hang from one?" They laughed again. They could not contain their joy.

A swarm of SAR members caught the stretcher and lowered Annette gently to the ground. Once unhooked, the helicopter flew away again, off to retrieve the dogs. They lifted the stretcher onto a gurney and there was a roar from the gathering crowd. They wanted to let Annette know they were there and also wanted to show the rescuers their appreciation.

Once she was in, the ambulance drove up to Marcel and Gabrielle and they climbed in. Family and friends cheered as the doors closed and the ambulance drove away. Annette was stable enough to have the two of them ride with her in the back all the way to the hospital.

There were quiet tears as the three hugged each other. Annette was stunned, completely unaware of all the hubbub. She couldn't grasp the scope of the rescue efforts and hadn't realized there even WAS a rescue effort. She thought Marcel had hired a helicopter to look for her, but that was all.

Little did she know the whole world was watching with bated breath…

Epilogue

While Annette was being transferred to the hospital with her husband and daughter, the three dogs were air lifted out of the bush along with some of the rescuers. They were greeted by the crowds, and of course their tearful owners. Poor Chloe was very confused when she couldn't find her family, but she was quickly whisked away by Nadine and brought to her vet who gave her a clean bill of health. It was recommended all the dogs eat light rations including no raw eggs for one week, in case they had parasites from drinking dirty water.

Roxy had raw patches where her legs rubbed against her body and the spots she was nervously licking. Fortunately, the raw patches healed quickly. Bubba had no obvious signs of trauma, though he does not stray too far from Annette on their hikes anymore.

In the ambulance, after a quick reunion with Marcel and Gabrielle, the paramedic continued ministering to Annette while they drove to Royal Columbian Hospital. Annette did not have a hint of pink on her skin as all her blood had moved to her core to protect her organs. Along with her shock and hypothermia, this was also a sign of her body shutting down. This also meant the paramedic was unable to put an IV into her arm or even get a pulse, but Annette assured her she was still alive.

Once in the emergency ward she was treated for dehydration and muscle trauma. Rhabdomyolysis, or just "Rhabdo", is a condition where muscle tissue dies, releasing substances into the blood which can cause kidney failure unless treated quickly. The treatment is simply flushing the body out with fluids through an IV. She would get frequent blood tests to monitor her recovery over the next five days.

Annette was visited by her out of town family in the emergency ward leading to another tearful reunion. She spent a sleepless night at the main ambulance entrance to emergency, watching many other patients being rushed in for emergency treatments. The horrific sights and sounds of that night were broken up by receiving many first responders and hospital staff's congratulations or simple thumbs up.

On the second day Annette was thankful to have moved from her emergency department curtained area to a proper room where she could begin to rest and recover. She spent the remainder of her five days in the hospital in a constant cycle of sleeping, physio therapy, and visitors. The highlight of her visitors was when Roxy and Chloe were first allowed to greet her. Both dogs could not have been happier to see her and covered her in many doggie kisses. Chloe had not been her normal self since the rescue, but when she saw Annette again, finally knowing she was safe, she started to get back to normal, and spent most of Annette's remaining hospital time at her bedside.

Marcel's days were spent running back and forth to the hospital, balancing Annette's need for company with her need for rest. Marcel also spent a considerable amount of time with the press who would not be satisfied until they finally got a chance to talk to Annette.

On day four, Annette took her first steps and on day six, she was released from the hospital. Once she was released there was a scramble for the press to have their time with Annette to get the story from her perspective. Marcel wheeled Annette's wheelchair by the media tent on their way to the van, and Annette gave them a brief statement.

As exhausting as that day was for her, when she learned that the Coquitlam SAR team was meeting that night for a 'lessons learned' session specifically regarding her rescue, she was determined she would not be left out. She dressed into street clothes and, using a borrowed walker, made her way into the SAR offices to greet and personally thank about 30 volunteers. It was an extremely emotional time for everyone in the room and it gave Annette and Marcel a private opportunity to thank those amazing ladies and gentlemen for their service to their family and to the community as a whole.

Later that same week, again using her walker, Annette and Marcel attended an Adventure Smart (a national prevention program for outdoor enthusiasts) presentation to promote safety when using the back country. Annette gave a very raw, emotional summary of what happened to her on that fateful day. Since then, Annette and Marcel take every opportunity to highlight the amazing work Search and Rescue organizations do, as well as promote personal safety to friends and other hikers.

A few weeks later, Annette and Marcel met with Richard Stewart, the Mayor of Coquitlam. He shared with them that shortly before Annette was found, the SAR people had been discussing changing the search to "recovery". Instead of teams walking 20 meters apart and doing a sound sweep (whistling and calling expecting to hear a response), they would walk 5 meters apart and look for a body.

Today Annette is back out in the back country, enjoying the tranquility of the forest with her beloved dogs. She never ventures into the forest without the Ten Essentials (see Appendix A), and tells everyone who talks to her regarding her incident about what they need to carry with them when out for a hike. She is also much better prepared with a GPS tracker, thanks to Island Communications Ltd. and Globalstar Canada.

Support your local Search and Rescue.

If you think it can't happen to you, you're wrong.

Acknowledgements

Annette and Marcel would like to thank the many people who helped them in their time of need:

To all the family and friends who traveled to be close or prayed and supported from a distance.

A special thanks to those who sat for hours with Marcel, wishing they could do more, but doing more than they could imagine just by holding him up when he needed you most.

Thank you to all the friends and neighbors in the community, for all the food and gifts you brought over to the house, and for all the cards and wine left at the front door.

Thank you to all the people we met on the street whose hugs meant so much to aid our healing and to confirm our faith in people.

Thank you to the news reporters Marcel met who showed him nothing but respect.

Last, but far from least, thank you to the first responders and Search and Rescue volunteers for your dedication, professionalism, and passion for what you do. So many people took time out of their personal lives for no other reason than to help someone in need. You are truly heroes in every sense of the word and will be in our hearts and minds always.

Appendix A

Before you leave for a hike, please ensure you have the following TEN ESSENTIALS with you:

1. Flashlight and spare batteries (or solar powered equivalents)

2. Extra food and water

3. Extra clothing

4. Map, compass, GPS or other navigational aid – keeping it in a large ziplock bag allows you to read it while keeping it dry

5. Fire starter (matches or lighter and some paper will do)

6. First Aid kit (just a few essentials)

7. Emergency shelter (even a garbage bag will do!)

8. Sun protection (sunscreen, a hat, sunglasses)

9. Pocket knife

10. Signalling device (whistle, mirror, flashlight, satellite radio, etc.) – obviously a cell phone is great, but sometimes they won't work if you're too far from towers. Take a spare battery or solar powered charger just in case it does work.

For full details on these items as well as other useful information, please visit the Coquitlam SAR website here:

www.coquitlam-sar.bc.ca/wilderness-education/ten-essentials/

For further outdoor preparedness information, please visit the Adventure Smart pages at:

https://www.adventuresmart.ca/about/about.htm

Most importantly, pack along some common sense:

- Tell someone where you are going
- Know which way is north, and which way points to civilization
- Know where you are headed and where the landmarks are

- If you get lost, stay put
- Make noise to keep wildlife away
- Make shelter – a lean-to with branches over it will be dryer than sitting in the rain
- Do not follow the sun, but remember it rises in the east and sets in the west
- Remember this simple rule: moss grows mostly on the north side of the tree in the northern hemisphere and the south side of the tree in the southern hemisphere

Resources

The Coquitlam SAR's full report on Annette's rescue is here:

www.coquitlam-sar.bc.ca/2017/11/three-dog-night-rescue-westwood-plateau/

There you will find much more information, including a description of the location, a full list of all SAR teams who contributed to the search, and news clips which aired at the time.

Contour and area maps can be found at the Coquitlam City site here:

www.coquitlam.ca/city-services/city-maps.aspx

Jon Lavoie Photography

https://www.themomentitclicks.ca/

Annette's Facebook page

https://www.facebook.com/AnnettesDoggieDaycare/

Photos

Annette with Roxy (left) and Chloe (right). This is precisely where her van was found. Photo by Anne Bruinn

Roxy

Bubba

Chloe

Photo by Annette

Searchers gathered around the Command Truck on the first night.

Photo by Marcel.

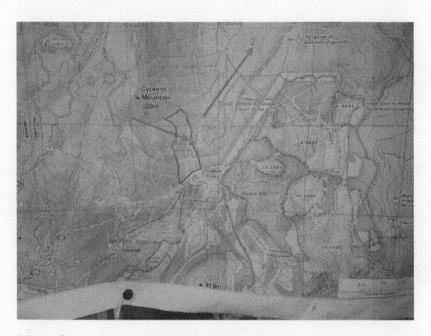

Map of search areas. Photo by Marcel.

Annette being lifted out with the longline. Photo taken from North Shore Search and Rescue Facebook page.

The dogs being harnessed in preparation for rescue. Photo taken from North Shore Search and Rescue Facebook page.

Annette arriving via longline. Source: Jon Lavoie Photography

Annette headed for the ambulance. Source: Jon Lavoie Photography

L to R: Janette, Marcel, and Maurice Poitras, sharing good news. Source: Jon Lavoie Photography

L to R: Gerald, Marcel, and Andy Poitras, waiting for Annette's arrival. Source: Jon Lavoie Photography

Aidon delivering Bubba to his owner, Tina. Source: Jon Lavoie
Photography

Media interviewing Marcel (not visible). Source: Jon Lavoie Photography

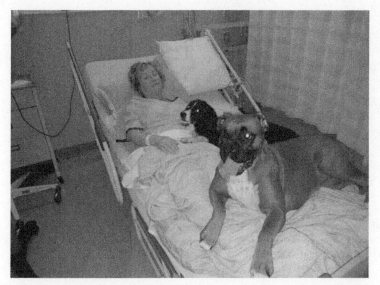

Annette in hospital with special visitors Chloe and Roxy. Photo by Marcel.

Annette and Chloe with the SAR members who found them (L to R): Darren Timmer (Coq SAR), Marcel, Annette, Stew Schulte (Surrey SAR), Aidon Pyne (Coq SAR), Christie Falk (CFV SAR), and Chloe the dog in the front. The 5th person on the rescue team was Toby Stahl (not pictured.) Photo by Marcel.

Annette with SAR members (L to R): Shayla Doble (South Columbia SAR), Steve Chapman (Coquitlam SAR), Kira M'Lot (Surrey SAR), Envy the dog, Andrew Wallwork (Surrey SAR). Photo by Marcel.

Aidon and Annette. Photo by Marcel.

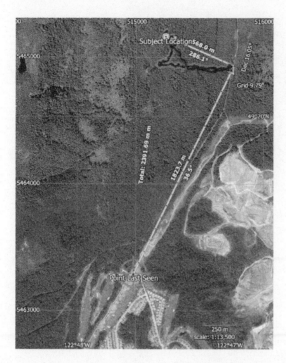

SAR map showing Annette's location at the time of rescue. Source: Coquitlam SAR

Coquitlam SAR Manager Michael Coyle working inside the Command Vehicle. Photo by Paul Dixon.

L to R: Michael Coyle, Jarrett Lunn (Talon pilot), Al Hurley, Steve MacDonald

SAR manager Ian MacDonald. Photo supplied by Ian MacDonald.

THANK YOU!

Made in United States
North Haven, CT
04 May 2023